Realty
Blogging

Realty Blogging

Build Your Brand and Outsmart Your Competition

Richard Nacht
and
Paul Chaney

McGraw-Hill

New York / Chicago / San Francisco / Lisbon
London / Madrid / Mexico City / Milan / New Delhi
San Juan / Singapore / Sydney / Toronto

The *McGraw·Hill* Companies

1 2 3 4 5 6 7 8 9 0 DOC/DOC 0 9 8 7 6

ISBN-13 978-0-07-147895-3
ISBN-10 0-07-147895-7

This publication is designed to provide accurate and authoritative information in regard to the subject matter covered. It is sold with the understanding that neither the author nor the publisher is engaged in rendering legal, accounting, or other professional service. If legal advice or other expert assistance is required, the services of a competent professional person should be sought.
>   —*From a Declaration of Principles jointly adopted by Committee*
>   *of the American Bar Association and a Committee of Publishers.*

McGraw-Hill books are available at special quantity discounts to use as premiums and sales promotions, or for use in corporate training programs. For more information, please write to the Director of Special Sales, McGraw-Hill Professional, Two Penn Plaza, New York, NY 10121-2298. Or contact your local bookstore.

Library of Congress Cataloging-in-Publication Data

Nacht, Richard.
Realty blogging : build your brand and outsmart your competition /
by Richard Nacht and Paul Chaney.
        p.   cm.
Includes bibliographical references.
ISBN 0-07-147895-7 (pbk. : alk. paper)
1. Real estate business—Blogs.   2. Real estate agents—Blogs.
3. Internet marketing.   I. Chaney, Paul, 1955–   II. Title.
HD1380.6.N33   2006
333.3068'8—dc22
                                        2006019832

To the many thousands of real estate bloggers.

Contents

Foreword

As one given to the rigorous study of the most powerful trends that dominate the real estate brokerage industry, I can state with confidence that during the last decade, very few change indicators have made such a significant and potentially long-lasting impact as technology. This is true for several reasons.

The first reason that springs to mind is its raw evolutionary speed. Many scientists believe that various species evolved over ancient millennia, and while this theory may be forever debated, the clearest, most accurate, and very real evolution that few question is the rapid advancement of technological innovations.

The second reason is the extent of technology's application potential as it continues to influence almost every facet of the industry. Some people even believe that technology may cause the total reengineering of the home buying and selling process.

A recent technology innovation that is starting to infiltrate real estate is blogging. Until relatively recently, Web logs (blogs) were viewed as nothing more than a curiosity, a kind of quasi-voyeuristic method of online journaling, a cultlike phenomenon or faintly embarrassing hobby. This is evidenced by the fact that even as I type such words as *Web log, blog,* and *bloggers,* Microsoft Word 2003 fails to recognize them.

In 2004, however, blogs unexpectedly vaulted into the forefront of major media, and today there are thought to be more than 50 million bloggers contributing on some kind of regular basis—a community that grows by the thousands every single day.

Blogging is rapidly developing into an instrument whose purpose, among others, is to establish an online presence, improve visibility, build a sense of community, maintain an open dialogue for clients and prospects, and offer valuable information—all of which is accomplished in a facade-less, unfiltered, much more candid way.

Therefore, by definition, blogging has a huge potential in real estate—for both brokers and agents. It is another untapped, powerful tool for the tech-savvy agent, another high-tech weapon in the real estate sales arsenal that should be used in tandem with the myriad Internet-related innovations such as Web sites, search engine optimization, and video and audio broad-casting, to strengthen the agent's overall marketing package and enable him or her to present a home sale or purchase experience that leaves client expectations in the dust.

As more traditional marketing avenues and vehicles continue to lose market share to their digital cousins, the real estate industry would be wise to gain as much understanding as we can about all the potential advantages inherent in the organic World Wide Web and all the new strategies, including blogging. Richard and Paul expertly detail and clarify this new phenomenon for real estate professionals in this new book. When you finally put it down and decide to embrace blogging—visit RealBlogging.com, the official blog site of the real estate industry.

Embrace, explore, and engage it. Conquer its intricacies, share in its knowledge base, maximize its huge potential, and then set a path to become the real estate blogging authority in your local market.

Stefan J. M. Swanepoel
CEO, RealtyU Group, Inc.
June 2006

Preface

*Blogging has hit the real-estate industry, . . . and it just may upend
a marketplace known for inefficiency and restricted information.*

CNN Money, January 2006

The real estate marketing landscape is in a state of flux. Tried and true offline techniques such as cold calling, old-fashioned farming, and conducting open houses just won't cut it in the twenty-first century. Marketing efforts such as these can only be part of the means for attracting new clients. Internet-based tools must be part of your marketing efforts if you expect to succeed in the new online competitive real estate sales market.

According to Edelman public relations (PR) strategist Steve Rubel, the marketing disciplines we know and love—the very ones that carried our careers forward—are dying. In Figure 1 he presents the old versus the new—and necessary—marketing tool kits.

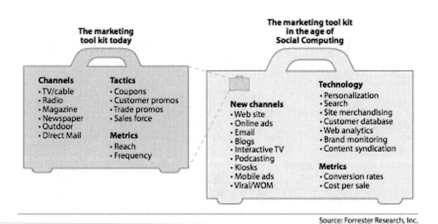

Figure 1. Twenty-first century marketing tool kit.

According to the 2006-2007 *Swanepoel TRENDS Report,* Internet technology has significantly changed the way the real estate marketplace operates and is one of the top 15 trends affecting the real estate industry. It is suggested in this report that brokers and agents can expect much greater benefits from technology as an "increased wave of innovation and the continued development of existing technology flood the market" (www.RealEstateTrendsReport.com).

As this Preface was being written, Google introduced, with its usual lack of fanfare, "Google Real Estate" (this is not an official name but one being used by online commentators). When you search for *real estate* or *homes for sale* or some similar language, a new option to search real estate properties appears on the search results page (Figure 2).

By entering property search data, which can be refined to include price, bedrooms, bathrooms, and more, you are shown thumbnail photos of properties alongside a Google local map. As seen in Figure 3, more property data are revealed when you click on the location of the property on the map.

The properties currently in the database appear to be self-served by users (e.g., all the properties located in Princeton, New Jersey, as of this writing were posted by a single Realtor). At the very least, this should suggest to you that the real estate marketing landscape is changing rapidly.

There is no question that Realtors are aware of the potential of the Internet. The *2005 Use of Technology Survey* issued by the California Association of Realtors stated, "Realtors are becoming more technologically savvy and have integrated many different technological tools into their real estate business and the real estate transaction." As evidence, the survey reported that 90 percent of Realtors have high-speed Internet connections, 46 percent use e-mail as their primary form of communication with clients,

Figure 2. Google "Real Estate."

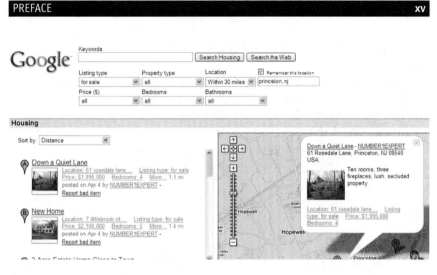

Figure 3.   Google "Real Estate" results.

61 percent post listings to their own Web sites, and 67 percent find the Internet extremely or very important in the marketing and promotion of their business (we have to wonder how the other 33 percent are getting by). Very telling is the final statistic from this report—*"33% of realtor business is coming from the Internet."*

Here's another statistic that absolutely validates the importance of the Internet for real estate marketing. In the most recent study available on the topic, the National Association of Realtors reported that 77 percent of home buyers use the Internet during their home search (*2005 National Association of Realtors Profile of Homebuyers and Sellers*).

These statistics are remarkable considering that Internet technology is still in its infancy when it comes to real estate marketing. It is estimated that more than one-third of all real estate transactions are being generated online, so it is easy to see why Internet marketing is such a crucial tool for Realtors. One of the most innovative Internet technology tools now being deployed by Realtors is Web logs, or *blogs.*

While most Realtors undoubtedly have heard the term *blog,* at this point, some actually may not be sure what a blog really is. Some of their teenage children might use a blog as a way to chronicle their daily activities on sites such as MySpace.com. Some might have seen a high-profile celebrity blog about his or her career and personal life or a political pundit rant on the latest doings inside the beltway.

Can these "personal online journals and diaries," as blogs have been thought of traditionally, really be used as a marketing tool for your real estate business? Can they improve your chances of generating more leads and actually result in more transactions? You bet they can—if you know how to use them.

The purpose of this book is to help Realtors do just that. We will present an arsenal of 10 strategic benefits that blogs can provide and back those up with real-life stories of Realtors who are using blogs to increase their income. Full transcripts of the interviews and podcasts are available on our Web site, www.realtybloggingbook.com.

Acknowledgments

Writing *Realty Blogging* took the efforts of a number of people. I thank Paul Chaney for his coauthorship, without which the book could not have been written. Our approach was very collaborative, with Paul providing much of the original content, which I then made relevant to effective real estate marketing. As is often the case within our company, Paul provided the soul of the material.

Words cannot express the gratitude I have for the patience and encouragement of my wife, Doreen, and our children, Christopher, Michelle, Joshua, Benjamin, Lauren, and Hannah. For extended periods of time, they were kind enough to leave me to my writing, which required great focus. Without their understanding and appreciation of the effort required, I could not have accomplished this undertaking. I am truly blessed to have such a wonderful family. Additional thanks go to my son-in-law, Chris Bubny, who has been instrumental (along with Christopher, Michelle and Joshua who also work with me) in evidencing the truth of the claims we make in this book regarding effective blog marketing through creating, managing, and editing very successful blog platforms that we have built.

I also would like to thank my parents, Sandy and Lyn Nacht, for their feedback and input regarding this book. More important, their guidance has led me to where I am in life.

I am also grateful to our editor, Dianne Wheeler. Her advice and direction created a book far better than we could have accomplished on our own.

Richard Nacht
Princeton, New Jersey

A few colleagues told me that writing a book would be some of the hardest work I would ever do. They were correct. It was a labor of love that could not have been completed without the help of some people who are especially deserving of thanks.

First, I want to thank the many bloggers who over the years have taught me so much about how to use the medium of blogging as a tool for business communications. This book is a tribute to you—your insight, your willingness to share ideas freely, and your encouragement.

I want to express my heartfelt appreciation to my wife, Amie, for her patience and support while I was sequestered those many hours attempting to meet writing deadlines. Without her encouragement, this dream would never have become a reality. To my sons, Alan and Jonathan, I express equal thanks. I hope *Realty Blogging* gives them yet another reason to be proud of their dad. I also would like to express my gratitude to my parents, Clarence and Jean Chaney, who taught me the value of hard work and the belief that I should set my sights on lofty goals.

I wish to thank our editor, Dianne Wheeler, who first approached us about writing this book. Her enthusiasm for this project and persistence in keeping us focused on achieving the best possible result kept us motivated. Without her, this book would never have been written.

Last, let me thank my coauthor, Richard Nacht. I may have provided the skeleton around which *Realty Blogging* was written, but he added the sinew and muscle. Thanks to his influence, I am a better writer. More important, thanks to his friendship I am a better man.

Paul Chaney
Lafayette, Louisiana

Introduction

Real estate blogs are the most exciting innovation in real estate in some time—connecting consumers to valuable information through an exciting and easy-to-use new medium. Real estate and blogs were made for each other. Real estate is local, personal, and emotional, just like blogs.

Blogs are made for fragmented, discreet, and almost one-on-one conversations. Realtors are in the overcommunication business: It is how they find new business and how they coach consumers over the hump of making the biggest investment decision of their lives.

It is not unusual, then, that more and more real estate professionals are finding blogs to be a powerful way to communicate. They are instant. They are localized. They are easy to use. And—the public loves blogging. Realtors are finding their distinct voices with blogs and are delivering routine posts that capture the interest of local home owners, borrowers, buyers, and sellers.

As we know, real estate professionals often use the term *farm* to describe their market area. It is an area too small for a ZIP code but large enough to make a living if the agent focuses exclusively on selling real estate in that area. Central to a Realtor's success is intense but valuable communication with prospects in his or her farm. As consumers have become more savvy about their real estate transactions, they are looking for more local insight, color commentary, and market information. They view information as a way to protect their investment and the best way to make wise choices about future real estate purchases.

For the last decade, consumers have been searching the Web for relevant information such as home listings, property records, home loans, school test scores, apartments for rent, and a wealth of other data. Such information weaves a valuable foundation of insight that contributes to smart decisions. However, while data are central to making informed choices, pure data are missing analysis, interpretation, and insight. Blogs fill that gap, particularly when the blogger is informed and posts on a routine basis.

In this new book, *Realty Blogging*, Richard Nacht, founder and CEO of Blogging Systems, and Paul Chaney, vice president of marketing, make the connection between these radically different worlds. They show readers how to leverage this remarkable new technology to make a difference in their communities and to find new customers and communicate more effectively with existing ones. Their writing is crisp, to the point, and actionable. Just as a good blog should be, they are passionate, and their voices are convincing and inviting.

Brad Inman
Inman News

Realty
Blogging

1

Blogging as a Strategic Real Estate Marketing Tool

Blogs are telling it like it is at the street level.
—BRAD INMAN
"Inman News"

What is a *blog?* Technically speaking, a blog is an easy-to-use Web-based content management system. It is a software platform that allows people with little or no technical background to publish, maintain, and update content. The activity of updating a blog is known as *blogging,* whereas someone who keeps a blog is a *blogger.* Entries written to the blog, called *posts,* are arranged in reverse chronological order, with the most recent additions featured at the top of the page. Readers of blogs also can comment on the posts. The result is an online dialogue on any topic of interest.

What makes a blog so unique compared to a typical Web site, message board, or e-mail application is the balanced combination of *technology* and *personality.* Blogs beg to be written in an informal, punchy, and shall we say *authentic* tone of voice, something Internet pioneer Doc Searls called an "e-mail to everyone." A well-written blog reflects the passions, biases, thoughts, and judgments of the writer. It has heart as well as substance.

Take, for example, Grow-a-Brain.com, a blog by real estate broker Hanan Levin (www.growabrain.typepad.com/growabrain). It is a fun,

March 19, 2006

The Yogurt Dispute

The price of paradise. What makes a Bel-Air estate worthy of a $53-million listing price instead of, say, a mere $38 million?

Real Estate Commissions Under Pressure. Steven Levitt (Author of Freakonomics) says their standard six-percent commission may become a thing of the past. The Internet is putting pressure on the fees that agents have become accustomed to

Real Estate Rap Song from Miami Realtor Phyllis D. Huguenin

World's largest tree house, in Alnwick Castle, Scotland

Amish neighbors take just one day to rebuild home destroyed by twister

Yogurt dispute hits a brick wall

Many More Unusual Real Estate Stories Here

March 19, 2006 in **Real estate | Permalink | Comments (2) | TrackBack**

Figure 1-1. Post from Hanah Levin's Grow-a-brain blog.

eclectic mix of information, some of which has to do with real estate and some of which does not. However, it is precisely the nature of the posts that make the blog a unique and widely read destination site. Not only does Levin's blog inform, but it also gives the reader insight into Levin's personality and interests. The sample blog in Figure 1-1 helps the reader "know" Levin better. To read his blog is to know him better. Levin uses his mix of real estate know-how and personality to create a harmonious flow between selected business and personal topics. The result is a natural traffic generator for his company's Web site.

However, personality and style alone are not enough to convey fully the power of blogs. We have to go back to the technology side to complete the picture.

BLOGS AND TECHNOLOGY

Blog technology provides an ability to do something no other content management medium does as well, and that is to stimulate conversation. Blog readers have the ability to comment on what you have written and have those comments appear on the site. They can ask questions, state opinions, tell stories, or relate a particular point of view.

The blogger then can respond either directly on the blog through a comment of his or her own or via an e-mail. Blogs enable dialogue between you and a client or prospect to enhance the opportunity to cultivate a long-term relationship substantially. This benefit alone offers great marketing potential.

The way blog technology was created makes blogs of particular value. Veteran blogger and author Rebecca Blood says that blogs are "native to the Web." She adds, "Everything about them—their format, their reliance on links, their immediacy, their connections to each other— is derived from the medium in which they were born. They are of the Web itself." What she means is that blog architecture and structure take advantage of the way the Web itself is built so that they maximize the benefits available, all of which we'll describe throughout this book.

Blogs are not only native to the Web; they are also changing the business end of the landscape. Blogs provide a low-cost, high-results tool for community building, competitive differentiation, marketing, sales, customer relations management (CRM), media contacts, and corporate collaboration. Plus, blog software is much simpler to use than what is required for Web sites, so any individual or organization can set up and maintain a blog. This simplicity of use and effectiveness in communication have resulted in a surge of new blog creation. According to David Sifry's *Technorati State of the Blogosphere* report from February 2006 (Figure 1-2), the size of the blogosphere is doubling every five-and-a-half months; it is now 60 times larger than it was three years ago. On average, a new blog is created every second of every day.

In May of 2005, *BusinessWeek* magazine carried this bold cover story:

Blogs Will Change the Way You Do Business. Look past the yakkers, hobbyists, and political mobs. Your customers and rivals are figuring blogs out. Our advice: Catch up . . . or catch you later.

The article went on to say:

Go ahead and bellyache about blogs. But you cannot afford to close your eyes to them, because they're simply the most explosive out-

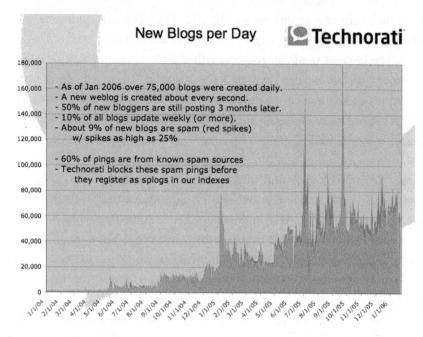

Figure 1-2.   Technorati State of the Blogosphere Report.

break in the information world since the Internet itself. And they're going to shake up just about every business-including yours. . . . Given the changes barreling down upon us, blogs are not a business elective. They're a prerequisite.

Do you have any doubt that this also applied to Realtors? If you do, then consider this quote from *CNNMoney* from January 2006:

Blogging has hit the real-estate industry, . . . and it just may upend a marketplace known for inefficiency and restricted information.

Imagine the blacksmith at the turn of the twentieth century. He's busy in his shop, steadily hammering a broken wagon wheel back into shape. Suddenly, in the distance, he hears a sound like nothing he has ever heard in his entire life. The sound could best be described as rhythmic sputtering peppered by occasional gunfire. Curiosity wraps him like a blanket, and the blacksmith cannot resist peering out the door of his shop only to gaze on something his eyes have never seen before—something he later learns is called a *motorcar.* Snickering at this mechanical monstrosity, the blacksmith returns to his work, never realizing the future had just passed in front of him, a future that will have a major negative impact on his business.

Will you respond like that blacksmith or be savvy enough to realize that blogging is the future of Internet marketing and understand the dramatic impact it can have on the way you do business? Even more to the point, will you join in this blogging (r)evolution?

From our perspective, not since Procter & Gamble invented branding back in 1931 has there been so much excitement about a fresh model for doing business. Blogs have a uniquely effective track record for results. Blogs put a human face on business leaders, companies, products, and services that surely will enhance the value proposition of you and your company to prospects. So let's get down to business.

TEN STRATEGIC BENEFITS

This book is framed around 10 strategic benefits of blogging. Each chapter addresses one particular benefit and will feature one or more real estate bloggers who are experiencing the effects of that benefit on their business.

Search Engine Marketing

Simply stated, blogs are search engine magnets. It's not that search engines seek out blogs specifically; they don't know the difference between a blog and a more traditional Web site. However, blogs *will* give you an increased presence on major search engines such as Google and Yahoo! The search engines are drawn to your blog because blogs contain the kinds of data that search engines look for, and the reasons will be enumerated in this chapter.

Direct Communications

We live in an age when people don't want to be talked at; they want to be spoken with. Blogs provide a way for you to speak directly and honestly with prospects and customers and provide a means through which they can talk to you. Blogging is less about sending a controlled, contrived sales message and much more about engaging in honest, open communication.

Brand Building

Blogs can become a major new channel through which you draw attention to your brand. Blogs let you tell the story of your brand over and over again, allowing your customers to become both familiar and comfortable with it. You know the old adage, "Tell them what you're going to tell them, tell them again, and then tell them what you told them." Blogs give you the ability to do this in order to create a competitive advantage.

Competitive Differentiation

What makes your business different from your competitor down the street? How can you make a prospective customer understand that you have something better to offer or that you have the expertise and experience to make the home buying and selling process easier and to their financial benefit? Blogs give your readers insight into who you are, what your business is all about, and what makes you a more worthy candidate than your competitor. They enable you to tell your story—the story of your business—the way you would like it to be told!

Positioning Yourself as the Expert

Blogs give you a platform for articulating your viewpoints, demonstrating your knowledge, and evidencing your expertise on matters pertaining to your industry or community. Through blogs, you can express your wisdom and impress readers with the fact that you know your business and that they can trust you with theirs.

Relationship Marketing

It has always been our belief that people don't want to do business with businesses; they want to do business with people, preferably people they know. It's not unlike the old-time corner grocery or general store. Blogs allow you to build personal, long-lasting relationships with your customers that foster trust. All Realtors are familiar with the importance of "farming" as a way of generating activity. This chapter will show how the traditional farm, consisting of a group of homes in a particular geographic area, is now, through the use of blogging, entering an entirely new and exciting world of relationship building!

Exploiting the Niches

Blogs are very niche-driven tools. You can use them to fill exploitable niches, virtually shutting out your competitors. Blogs are well suited to creating your own market. For example, if your area of interest consists of targeting the Latino community, blogs can be written in Spanish and English so that your customers know that you are capable of conducting a transaction in Spanish. If your preference is the luxury market, you can share experiences that make the reader understand that *you* know *them* and their way of life. It doesn't matter what your target market is; blogs enable you to reach that target market more effectively.

Media and Public Relations

If getting media attention is important to you (and it should be), blogs are excellent tools to help you achieve that end. Expect the media to call you, not your competition. A Realtor associate of ours recently held a breakfast meeting with the contributing members of his community blog. Also attending the meeting was the publisher of his local newspaper, who incidentally was not a participant in the community blog. Imagine the publisher's surprise to find out that he had new competition—20 community members, from the local Chamber of Commerce to local charitable organizations to local sports teams, writing about their own activities within the community. Needless to say, the publisher quickly made it clear that he wanted in, and very shortly thereafter, the newspaper published a very complimentary article on the new community blog.

Lead Generation

While blogs are not lead-generation systems in the strictest sense, you will find them providing you with a consistent flow of leads at almost no cost.

By using all the tools we will share with you throughout this book, the leads from your blog not only will be consistent, but they also will be more qualified than those bought from online lead generators because you will have been engaging your readers in an ongoing dialogue.

Intranet and Project Management

Large brokerages and associations with large memberships can appreciate the need for an easy-to-use internal communications and content management system. Blogs fit the bill quite well. This may be one of the least known and most underutilized areas of blogs.

CONCLUSION

Blogging is relatively new to the real estate community. For this reason, we suggest that you think carefully about blogging but move quickly when you are ready because the "first movers" have a tremendous advantage. The first mover might not win—great content and effective blog tools are important—but by reading the rest of this book and implementing these tools, you will have the best chance of becoming *the* blogger of record for your target market.

2

Search Engine Marketing

[Y]ou cannot afford to close your eyes to them [blogs], because they're simply the most explosive outbreak in the information world since the Internet itself. And they're going to shake up just about every business-including yours. . . . Given the changes barreling down upon us, blogs are not a business elective. They're a prerequisite.

—BusinessWeek, May 2, 2005

In real estate it is often said that the three most important things are location, location, location. The same can be said of search engines. It makes all the difference for a Web site to be located on the front page of Google when a keyword query is performed in terms of both the traffic it receives and the number of leads and business acquired as a result.

In the current Internet marketing landscape, search engines have premium value. Research shows that up to 70 percent of all traffic to a given Web site comes through search engines, and as noted previously, 77 percent of home shoppers use the Internet during their home search. In order to build an effective Internet marketing strategy, focus on using methodologies and techniques that will attract the attention of search engines, particularly Google.

Although search engines have been around a long time, most real estate brokers and agents have yet to succeed in optimizing their Web sites sufficiently to be ranked highly in major search engines such as Google,

Yahoo!, and MSN. A blog is a wonderful tool to produce high search engine results. Blogging helps Realtors get the most "bang for their buck" when it comes to search engines.

SEARCH ENGINE VALUE

Hundreds of millions of Web pages exist on the World Wide Web, presenting information on virtually every topic imaginable. Cataloging and indexing those pages is the job of search engines. Without search engines like Google or Yahoo!, accessing such information in a timely manner would be almost impossible. Because of the vital role of search engines, capturing their attention is of extreme importance. There are two ways that this can be accomplished: search engine optimization and search engine marketing.

Generally speaking, *search engine optimization* (SEO) results are those obtained without having to be paid for, whereas *search engine marketing* (SEM) results are paid for. A huge advantage to using blogs is that they can produce high search engine results without having to pay for the costs associated with typical search engine marketing. This occurs when your site appears in the "organic" section of a search engine results page. The organic results are those that appear in the main column of the results

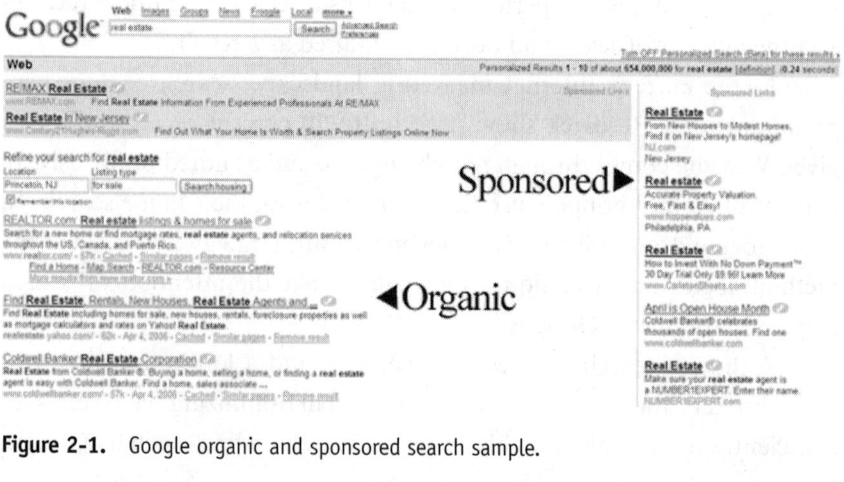

Figure 2-1. Google organic and sponsored search sample.

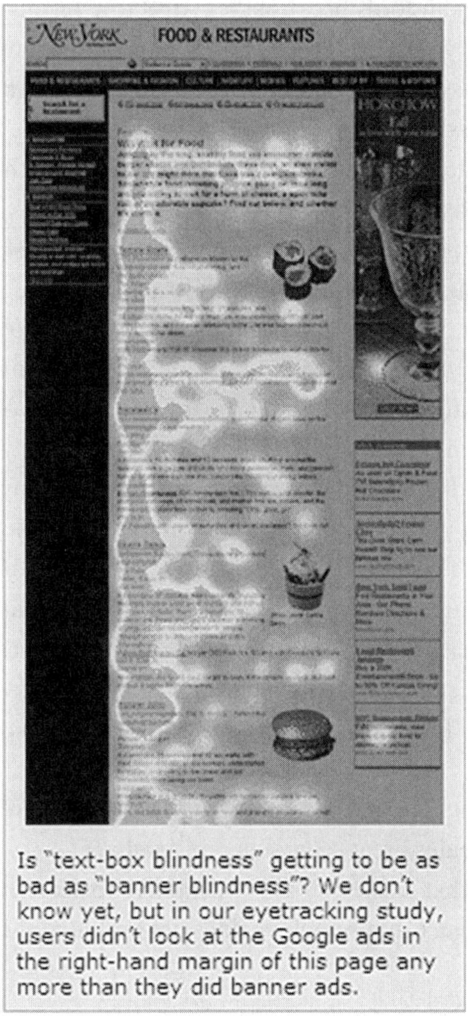
FOOD & RESTAURANTS
Is "text-box blindness" getting to be as bad as "banner blindness"? We don't know yet, but in our eyetracking study, users didn't look at the Google ads in the right-hand margin of this page any more than they did banner ads.

Figure 2-2. Eye tracking chart.
(Jakob Nielsen, Kara Pernice Coyne, "Eyetracking Web Usability," Nielsen Norman Group, www.nngroup.com/events/tutorials/eyetracking.html.)

page, below any sponsored links. (See Figures 2-1 and 2-2 for examples.) SEM results, in general, require payment for inclusion, such as sponsored links. These links appear most often as the first one or two listings on the search page, as well as, for Google, the listings off to the right-hand side of the page.

Blogs are great tools because their structure results in better organic (free) results for your site. This is particularly important because recent evidence suggests that the number of search visitors who click on sponsored links *is less than 20 percent.* This means that the vast majority of search visitors are clicking on the organic results—those where blogs results can be most effective.

Toronto broker Fraser Beach was one of the first Realtors to embrace blogging, having begun his blog, "Toronto at Home," in 2001 (http://toreal.blogs.com). Early on, he saw blogging as a way to create a stronger presence on the Internet through the value of search engines. "I only use two media for marketing, MLS and the Internet. I discovered that because of the treatment of blogs by search engines—particularly Google—it supported 'presence.' Blogging is a major component of my presence on the Internet." Beach understood very early the power of blogs for search engine optimization.

Following are two screen shots from a Google search. Figure 2-3 is for "Toronto Real Estate Blog." Figure 2-4, more meaningfully, is for "Toronto Real Estate." Beach's blog is listed as number one and number four, respectively (after the paid-for sponsored listings) out of 22,400,000 results!

These results are organic—not paid for. (Can there be any question that blogging creates great search engine results?)

What is it that makes blogs so attractive to search engines, particularly Google? It isn't that search engines are looking for blogs specifically.

Google   Web   Images   Groups   News   Froogle   Local   more »

toronto real estate blog   [Search]   Advanced Search
                                                Preferences

Web   Results 1 - 10 of about 2,210,000

Toronto at Home :: **Toronto's Real Estate Blog**
Toronto Real Estate Blog. List @ 0.5%. Find homes for sale in the Toronto area, updated
daily for Toronto and Durham Region.
toreal.blogs.com/ - 42k - Cached - Similar pages

Toronto Real Estate - Full service MLS for 3% - never more
Find Toronto Real Estate. MLS @ 3%. Homes for sale on the Toronto Real Estate Board
Multiple Listng Service. Toronto at Home Real Estate Blog.
toreal.blogs.com/durham/ - 22k - Cached - Similar pages

Figure 2-3.   Google search results for "Toronto Real Estate Blog."

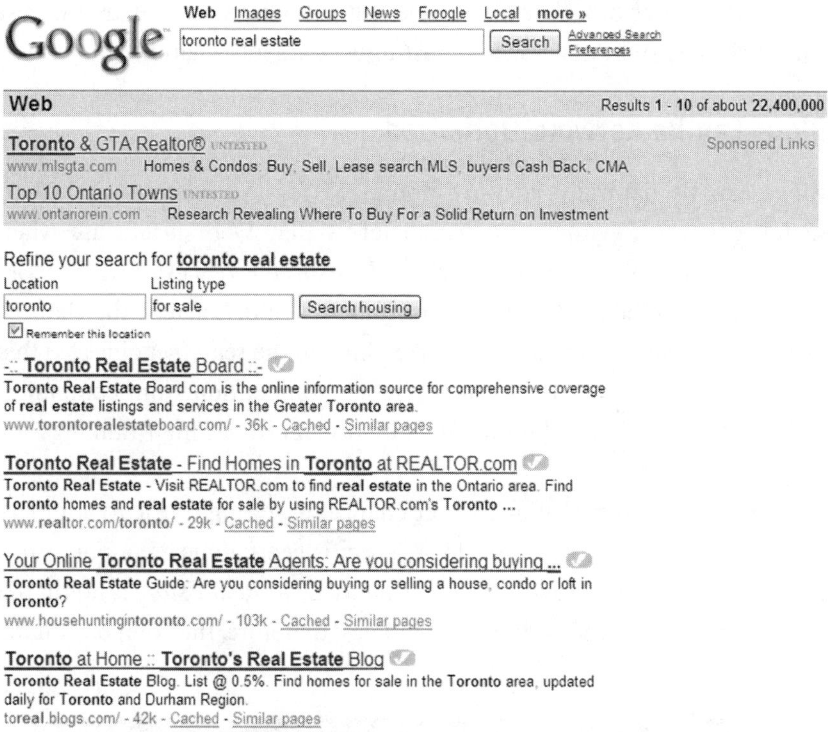

Figure 2-4. Google search results for "Toronto Real Estate."

A search engine can't tell the difference between a blog and a traditional Web site. It is simply that blogs contain the kinds of data that are especially alluring to search engines. Google doesn't care about Flash animation or graphics. What it wants is content in the form of words, and that is what blogs provide—words, and lots of them. Not only that, thanks to the way blogs format HyperText Markup Language (HTML), content is served up in a manner most appealing to the engines. Quite simply, blogs are *search engine magnets!*

Search Engine Optimization Benefits of Blogging

Blogs, by their very design, meet the current requirements for search engines and search traffic. Search engines need to deliver the latest information accurately, and search engine traffic wants the most accurate information now. Blogs are highly relevant in their niches and are the best sources online right now for the most up-to-date information.

Blogs Can Be Keyword-Optimized

Blogs can be naturally keyword-optimized for even greater appeal to search engines. *Keywords* are search terms that Web surfers use when searching for information or Web sites. For example, *real estate* is the most commonly searched for term in our industry. Unfortunately, the chances of your site, even a blog, getting ranked high in the search engines for this phrase are remote. There is just too much competition from companies with deep pockets spending millions of dollars to get high rankings for this general term.

You have a substantially better chance of getting traffic to your site by focusing your keywords on a local, specific geographic area. For example, a local search term such as *Lake County Ohio Real Estate* is not in the SEO plans of the large national brokerages; therefore, the competition for

---

EXPERT'S TIP ➤ How to Find Good Keywords

Want to know how popular your keywords are with the search engines or which keywords are more likely to provide you with positive search engine results? Here are some free keyword analysis tools:

- **Overture Keyword Selector Tool:** http://inventory.overture.com/d/searchinventory/suggestion/
- **Google Keyword Tool:** http://adwords.google.com/select/KeywordToolExternal
- **Cool SEO Tool:** www.webuildpages.com/cool-seo-tool/
- **Wordtracker (free trial):** www.wordtracker.com/
- **Digital Point Keyword Suggestion Tool:** www.digitalpoint.com/tools/suggestion/

Just remember that the most popular keywords are probably *not* the right ones for you to use in your blog-the competition for them is too great. Use localized keywords that you can "own" with proper keyword strategies, as outlined in this chapter.

a high ranking for this term is much less. According to an Overture.com keyword selector analysis for February 2006, there were 1,795,889 searches for *real estate. Lake County Ohio Real Estate* had 109 searches during the same period. Clearly, the numbers suggest that you should focus on local search terms.

Local search is fast becoming the ultimate goal of SEO. "Definitely more businesses, particularly service businesses, are using local search," says senior Yankee Group analyst Sanjeev Aggarwal. "They know people aren't looking in the Yellow Pages" (*BusinessWeek SmallBiz,* Spring 2006). According to Kelsey Group, a research company that focuses on electronic directories and local media, more than 50 percent of consumers used a search engine to find information about a local business in 2005. By using your localized keywords judiciously throughout your blog design and blog content, your blog easily can rank well for those keywords in the search engines without gimmicks or search engine tricks.

Blogs Have Search Engine–Friendly Code

Blogs are text-rich publishing tools, meaning that they contain more plain text than most Web sites. Unlike many Web sites, blogs are not encumbered with lots of poorly formatted HTML code, images, or Flash animations. Instead, they use a search engine–friendly code format called *Cascading Style Sheets* (CSS). Less code equals easier crawling by search engines and greater visibility and clarity of content. This "leanness" of code enables search engines to understand the topical nature of your blog better.

Blogs Get Crawled More Quickly

Blogs get crawled more quickly and more often. Because blogs are lean in terms of the underlying code used to produce them, search engine "spiders" can crawl your blog faster. Not only that, because blogs tend to be updated more frequently with fresh new content, search engine spiders visit them more often. This means that blogs get their content into search results in hours and days rather than weeks and months. In fact, there are search engines dedicated solely to blogs, such as Technorati.com (see Expert's Tip—Tag Your Posts for Technorati), that often can include new blog content in their results in just a few minutes. Think of fresh content as a new item on display in the window of a bricks-and-mortar storefront. Retail shops are always looking for new items to add to their displays to attract attention. Similarly, restaurants regularly change menus with a special of the day. Customers love seeing new things. So it is with the search engines-fresh, new content is a flare in the sky saying, "Come see me—I'm new!"

EXPERT'S TIP ➤ Tag Your Posts for Technorati

Tagging is the practice of Web users labeling content with specific terms that can be retrieved, shared, and searched for easily. Tags can be applied to text, graphics, photos—just about anything. According to *BusinessWeek* (February 28, 2005), the tagging trend "represents a new approach to organizing and finding information online, and industry watchers expect it to draw people away from the traditional net search offered by Yahoo! and Google Inc. Tagging won't replace Google et al. But people may turn to tags more frequently over time, reducing their use of established search engines." By tagging your content with relevant terms for Technorati, you will capture those searches taking place on Technorati while your competitors aren't.

Blogs Are Natural Link Builders

Hyperlinks are a Realtor's best friend for search engines' rankings. The more links you get, the better. The more relevant the link, the more importance that link has for search engine results. An inbound link from another Web site or blog is a vote of confidence in your content. It is like someone putting up a sign saying, "Go to this site; it's worth the trip." Blogs naturally generate inbound links, because in the world of blogs, it's the thing to do. Bloggers are part of a community, and linking to other worthwhile content is a normal part of participating in the "blogosphere." Great content is found by others in the world of blogs and linked to on a regular basis. Write good content, and you will get good inbound links.

Relevance Is Key

The key to search engine optimization (SEO) is one word—*relevance.* Business blog consultant Wayne Hurlbert, author of the "Blog Business World" blog (blogbusinessworld.blogspot.com), concurs:

> *Whether it is incoming links, PageRank levels, or positions in the search engine results pages, there is one common denominator, and that is the value that Google is placing on theme and topic related content. The watchword of the day, in the land of Google, is relevance.*

Blogs are a great way to connect to your market by adding an all-important theme and topically relevant content. This will tie your marketing efforts together and really get you noticed by the search engines! Hurlbert continues:

> *Blogs are regularly updated postings of information, usually related to the theme of a website, and include incoming and outgoing links on the same topics. Since the posts will be on topics related to the overall website theme and incoming links will arrive from similarly themed blogs, relevance is an obvious and natural result.*

Google's algorithm, which is the mathematical calculation that determines a site's position in the search results for any given keyword or phrase, has been revised to stress the importance of relevance. "In fact," says Hurlbert, "the Google algorithm could have easily been written with blogging in mind."

Because relevance is so important, your blog should niche itself around a single topic or a few select topics. With few exceptions, if a blog is all over the map in terms of topical content, it will not rank as well as if it is sharply defined.

Link Strategies and Tools

Search engine specialists are very well paid to help Web site owners reach that lofty plateau of a number-one (or first-page) ranking for a chosen number of keywords. At a conference we attended, a panel member noted that one of his clients was optimizing his site with over 100,000 keywords. Interestingly, blogs seem to find their way to the top on their own.

But what is it that causes one page to rise above another in the returns, and why do blogs seem to return so well? One reason is clearly that Google seems to have a particular fondness for blogs, and because it is the most popular search engine, we'll answer this question using Google's methodology as an example.

Google uses a measurement called *PageRank* to determine which sites show up and in what order. PageRank is a numeric value that represents how important a page is on the Web. Google figures that when one page links to another, it is effectively casting a vote for the other page. The more votes cast for a page, the more important that page must be. Also, the importance of the page that is casting the vote determines the importance of the vote itself. Google calculates a page's importance from the votes cast for it and the relative importance of each vote based on that page's own PageRank. The bottom line: The more pages from other Web sites and blogs that are linking to yours, the better, especially if those sites have a high PageRank themselves.

The beauty of blogs is that the technology inherent in almost every blog platform encourages such inbound linking. Blogs are built to naturally foster such interactivity, and there are a number of ways this works.

Links from Other Blog Posts

Blogs are all about engaging in conversation. They were never intended to be a one-way medium. Once you've gotten the attention of another blogger via a comment or trackback on his or her blog, a dialogue will begin. (A *trackback* is a method of communication between blogs, and it will be explained in more detail later in this chapter). As other bloggers write about a post on your blog, most will link to it. Search engine optimization specialist Lee Odden of Top Rank Online Marketing says that a "link in a blog post from another blog to your site is the best possible link you can get."

A link directed toward your blog is called a *backlink* or *inbound link*. As noted earlier, the number of these inbound links is an indication to the search engines of the popularity or importance of your site.

In blog nomenclature, this is called *link love.* Link love results in the acquisition of a special elixir called "Google juice"—a magic potion that will increase search engine results. Such links can be of inestimable value, especially if they come from a popular blogger whose site itself has a high volume of relevant inbound links. The more links and the higher the quality of those links, the higher your PageRank will be, and the better your search engine results will also be.

In addition, the relevance of the inbound links is important. If the inbound links come from sites that have content related to your site, these

---

EXPERT'S TIP ➤ Generate the Best Backlinks

Wouldn't it be great if you could have links to your blog from the top 10 real estate bloggers in the United States? The chance of you getting them isn't likely if those bloggers don't know who you are. The best way for them to learn about you and your blog is to leave relevant comments on their posts.

As soon as your blog is up and running and you have worthwhile content written, start commenting on the other bloggers posts, and why not start with the most popular sites—if you get a backlink, they'll be more valuable to you.

Here's our list of those to start with (some popular ones don't allow comments and aren't listed here):

Grow-a-Brain: http://growabrain.typepad.com/growabrain/real_estate_blogs/index.html
Rain City Guide: www.raincityguide.com/
Inman News Blog: www.inman.com/blogger/bradinman.aspx
RealBlogging: www.realblogging.com
The Walk-Through: http://walkthrough.nytimes.com/
RealtyBlogging: www.realtyblogging.com
Transforming Real Estate: http://jimkimmons.typepad.com/transforming_real_estate/2006/04/whats_your_ce_r.html
Flipping Frenzy: http://flippingfrenzy.com/serendipity/
Matrix: http://matrix.millersamuel.com/?p=304
Lenderama: http://reblog.mariah.com/

links are considered more relevant—contributing to the theme of your site—and therefore more valuable for purposes of ranking. It is generally believed that search engines prefer links built over time. This reduces the likelihood of someone gimmicking the system and creating lots of artificial links, hoping to get a quick kick in positive results.

A sound strategy to encourage traffic to your blog is to find popular bloggers who are addressing similar issues and place a comment on their posts. Then you also can write about their posts in your blog. It is important that your posts not be considered *spam*. The comments and posts created must be substantive and on-topic. The aim is to add value to the conversation, not simply to improve the PageRank.

Find other real estate bloggers, especially more popular ones, and leave salient comments on their posts. Write about things they've said in posts of your own, and create a trackback when possible. Invariably, some of these bloggers will take note and return the favor. Remember, it's Google juice that you want, and the best way to get it is via interaction with other bloggers in the blogosphere.

For the purposes of this chapter, we are focusing on the SEO value of links. Clearly, having links to your blog from other relevant and highly trafficked sites is important in itself. You can't build a blog and simply expect people to find your site without any "driving instructions." Having pointers to your site from other sites is a most effective way of getting visitors to your blog.

Blogrolls

Our experience with real estate bloggers is that they are a friendly group and are happy to link to your site either by commenting on content you've written or by placing your site in their blogroll. A *blogroll* is simply a list of links a blogger places on his or her blog. When a blogger places a link to your blog in his or her blogroll, he or she is recommending to his or her own readers that they visit your blog. If your writing is interesting and creative and you spend time communicating with other real estate bloggers, it is likely that you will create a good number of inbound blogroll links.

Following are examples of two blogrolls. Figure 2-5 is from "The Real Estate Blog," written by Fran Vernon and Rowena Emmett (http://franandrowena.blogspot.com). Figure 2-6 is from Jim Kimmons, Realtor, consultant, and author of the "Technology for Real Estate" blog, (www.technologyforrealestate.com).

CASE STUDY: *Chris Bubny*

A further example of the importance of blogrolls is Chris Bubny's "Realty Blogging" community blog (www.realtyblogging.com), a network of blogging evangelists writing on effective real estate blogging. The site went from inception and zero inbound links to over 100 inbound links within just 60 days after the blog went live. This was accomplished through a focused effort by Bubny and the blogging evangelists writing for the blog to communicate often and intelligently on real estate blogging with other real estate bloggers. This ongoing collaboration paid off for the site because it quickly rose in search engine rankings. Such an outcome would be practically impossible with a static Web site.

Comments, Trackbacks, and Backlinking

Two blog platform components already mentioned—comments and trackbacks—are used frequently by bloggers to communicate with one another. When you read a blog post, it is generally possible to leave a comment in response. That comment gets listed chronologically beneath the post itself. Most comment forms have three fields: one for name, one for e-mail address, and a field for the Uniform Resource Locator (URL) of the commenter's blog or Web site. In most cases, the name of the commenter will appear and be hyperlinked with the URL of his or her site when the comment is posted to the blog. This hyperlink connection is called a *backlink*.

Trackbacks are another way backlinking happens. Trackbacks are a technology that appears solely in blogs. *Trackbacks* are a way one blogger tells another blogger that he or she's been talked about. Following is an example of how a trackback can work:

**Real Estate Blogs
& other Blogs-Weblogs**

"Grow A Brain"

Blog Search Engine

Blogwise Directory

Blog Universe

Search4Blogs

The Octopus Files

Great New Mexico Homes

Blog Link List

Beautiful Santa Barbara Blog

LOCATION LOCATION LOCATION...

the Touchstone of Real Estate Properties

Chicago Real estate Blog

Hot Property Real Estate Blog

Investment Real Estate Blog

Portland Real Estate Blog

Preconstruction Real Estate Blog

Blog Rankings

TheREALTYgram Blogger

The CA Real Estate Law Blog

Wentachee Residential Real Estate Blog

Wentachee Investment Blog

Weblog Directory

Sarasota Real Estate News

Arizona Real Estate Blog

Eastern CT Real Estate Blog

Real Estate News Headlines

Realty Blogging

Sacramento Real Estate Blog

Oakland Real Estate Blog

Figure 2-5. Fran and Rowena's Blogroll.

REAL ESTATE
BLOG LINKS

REMBEX - Mortgage & Real Estate

Transforming Real Estate

Taos, NM Real Estate

Squidoo

Realty Blogging

NAR Tech Tips

Demo Real Estate Intranet

Broker Agent News

Figure 2-6. Jim Kimmon's Blogroll.

When a blogger reads a post on another blog and wants to comment about it in a post on her own blog, she can let that blogger know that she has done so by using a special link called a *trackback URL,* usually found just beneath the blog post she is referencing. All of the best blog platforms accommodate this technology.

The blogger copies that URL and pastes it into a special field on her blog posting user interface. When the post is published, the other blogger's site is *pinged,* and an excerpt of what she said appears under the other blogger's post. In the same manner as comments, a link back to the site is also included. In most blog platforms, the original blogger gets an e-mail with a notice that a comment or trackback has been created.

Figure 2-7 shows what a trackback link looks like at the end of a post from Hanan Levin's "Grow-a-Brain" blog.

If you were to click on the trackback link, you would be taken to a separate page within Levin's blog that includes the comments that have

The complete List of Real Estate Blogs as well as Grow-a-Brain's Extensive Real Estate Archives are Here

September 29, 2005 in **Real estate Blogs** | **Permalink** | **Comments (4)** | **TrackBack**

Figure 2-7. TrackBack link in post footer.

been made by other bloggers on their sites that reference this original post.

Search engines may not put as much weight on these types of links as others, such as a link within a blog post itself. This doesn't mean they shouldn't be used. In fact, comments and trackbacks are basic to creating any search engine marketing strategy with blogs.

The fact is that even if no such backlinking were taking place, comments and trackbacks have intrinsic value because they get the attention of the blogger with whom you are interacting. If I am writing about another blogger on my blog, then maybe he will write about me on his blog, and that is of utmost value. It is this type of community collaboration, the commenting on and discussion of topics with other bloggers, that can result in your blog becoming a "destination of choice" for your blog's topic.

In a recent post on the "Inman News" blog entitled, "Elephant in the Room," Brad Inman asked why Realtors and their commission structure were "under siege and whether this time around things were different." There were *over 300 comments* to Inman's post. Then, shortly thereafter, Inman posted the following:

> ### Help me out here
> *Why did my* "Elephant in the Room" *blog about real estate commissions prompt such an incredible response, quickly syndicated on the Web with more than 300 comments on the Inman Blog alone? Pro and con, it was overwhelming. Play armchair sociologist for a moment, give me your insight. Tipping point? Pile on?*

What happened? Another 16 comments, and here is a very telling one:

> *[B]ecause [now] we can comment with the advent of the blog.*

How many ways can you think of that you could create an ongoing conversation among your clients, prospects, and other industry participants that would generate 300+ responses? Blogs enable this kind of communication, community building, and ongoing collaboration.

As a final note, the best blog platforms allow you to moderate comments so that no inappropriate content reaches your blog site. In addition, the best blog platforms also include spam filters that prevent comment spam from reaching your blog site, so be sure to choose a blog platform that allows both comment moderation and spam control.

Links to Other Blog Posts

It's not only inbound links that make your blog a search engine magnet. Outbound links to other topically relevant blogs have impact as well. Search engine specialist Lee Odden, mentioned previously, encourages bloggers to link to other sites often. "The value of a post from a search engine perspective can be determined by who you are linking out to, as well as the content of your own site," Odden suggests. "If you have a blog post that takes a position and links to a site with relevant information, it adds value, as does creating a link out to an external authoritative resource, particularly if they have been indexed by Google already. Who you link to is important."

Fellow search engine specialist Wayne Hurlbert says that these context-sensitive blog links are especially valuable in three ways:

> *The first and obvious benefit is what accrues from any link, in the form of link popularity and transferred Google PageRank. The second benefit comes from the potentially keyword rich link anchor text from right in the post itself [anchor text is the actual word(s) used in the hyperlink itself; that is,* Lake County Ohio Real Estate *as a hyperlink creates value not only because of the link but also because of the words themselves]. Keywords are often found in those linked passages. The third benefit is from context. . . . Surrounding the link is usually very theme relevant content, containing similar important keyword phrases. That context ensures that the sending page is very theme relevant. Since bloggers tend to read and link to blogs focusing on their main area of interest, their outgoing links are most likely highly relevant.*

Linking is inherent to blogging philosophy and contributes to its power as a search engine marketing tool. As such, it's important to include links to other blogs and Web sites often in your posts. Be sure to take Hurlbert's advice and use keywords as the link text. Because you are most likely writing about a few select topics, those keywords will be surrounded by highly relevant content, thereby maximizing the power of your blog to attract search engine attention.

Implementing an outbound link strategy also pays off in a community sense, just as we described with comments and trackbacks. Linking to other bloggers, especially well-read ones (with high PageRank numbers), is very likely to get them to give your blog a read. This "favor" you've done for them, by giving them an inbound link to their site, is likely to at least get their attention and, if your content is relevant to them, could easily result in an ongoing conversation and hopefully your own return link. Do not forget—blogs have magic and power inherent in their structure, but the positive offline community building that results from blog interaction can be of the greatest value. Who knows where a kind word or complimentary observation could lead?

Community Blogs

Community blogs consist of multiple bloggers as compared to a site with a single blogger. The secret associated with multiblogger community sites for purposes of SEO is that blog communities create stronger search engine optimization leverage because each new post creates links that point to your main community site, to other community members, and to your regular business Web site as well, if you have one. With the proper use of keywords, links, and the tools discussed throughout this chapter, your own branded community blog can be a powerful marketing tool. Because of the cross-posting that takes place among community blogs, search engine results are improved dramatically for all the reasons addressed previously. A very important point, discussed in greater detail later in this book, is that this model contains content from all the participants and is not limited to a single person's content—thus reducing the need for a Realtor to spend more time than he or she might wish creating new content.

- -
CASE STUDY: *David Crockett*

As proof that community blogs work with regard to links to your regular business Web site, here is a screen shot from a Google search for *Lake*

County Ohio Real Estate. This search was done three months after Mentor, Ohio, Realtor David Crockett started his "Lake County Blog" (www.lake countyblog.com). Prior to the creation of Crockett's community blog, his business Web site did not appear in early pages of search engine results. Three months later, after creation of hundreds of links to his Web site from his community blog, his company Web site has achieved the highest reward of search engine optimization, a listing on page one (Figure 2-8)!

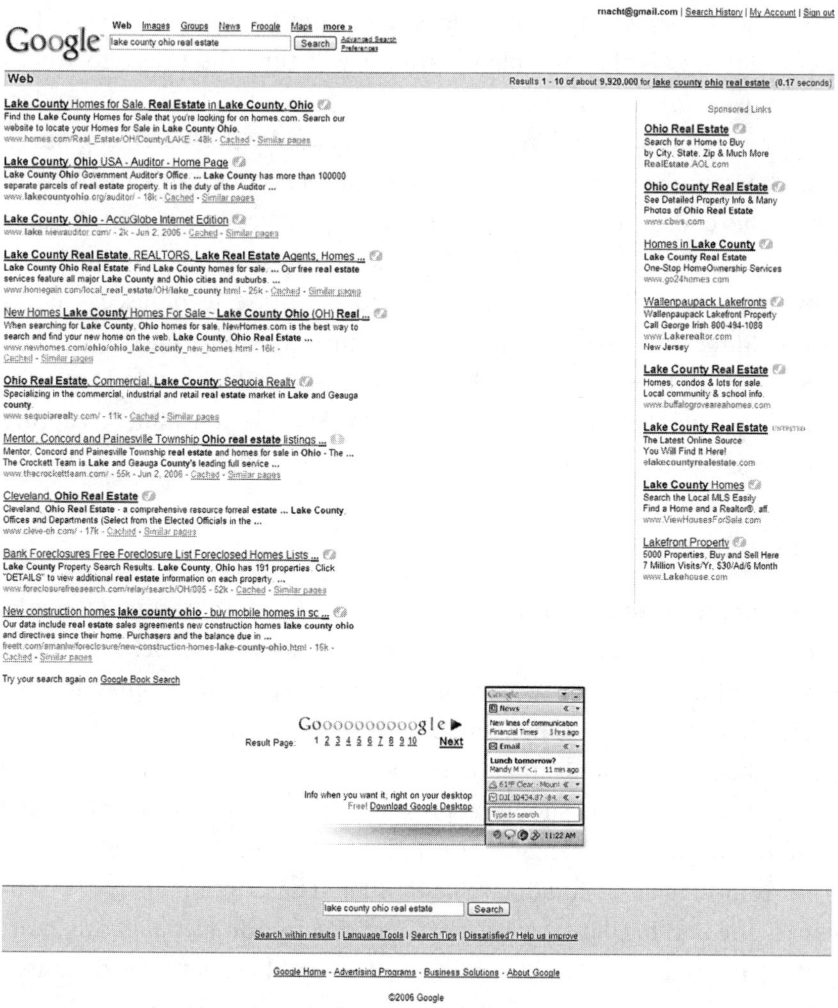

Figure 2-8. Google search results for "Lake County Ohio real estate."

TAGS AND PERMALINKS

While fresh content, relevance, and links—both inbound and outbound—play a significant role in why blogs rank well, they are not the only reasons. Blog post titles, header tags, and permalinks are equally significant.

Title Tag

Blog post titles are extremely important to search engine marketing success, so it's imperative that you title each of your blog posts properly. The reason for this is that the blog platform will turn the title into what's known as a *title tag*. A title tag is simply a piece of HTML code understood by the browser and, more important, used by the search engines to select content for its searching process (you do not need to know how to create this code; blog software does this automatically for you). Google puts a great deal of emphasis on the title tag. In fact, it is absolutely the most important place for a keyword or key phrase to be used—hands down. Make sure that you keyword-optimize the title, making it even more relevant to the engines. Thus "Lake County Real Estate Home for Sale" is a much better title than "Home for Sale" if you want to capture searchers looking for homes for sale in Lake County.

Header Tag

Furthermore, most blog platforms also wrap a *header tag* around the title, which further increases its value to search engines. A header tag can be thought of as the main section headers in a term paper—they tell the reader, in this case the search engines, what the major point of the site is (remember, we mentioned that blogs give search engines exactly what they want). This header tag should approximate the content in your title and reinforce for the search engines the topic of your site.

Your blog also should have keyword and description *metatags*. Similar to title and header tags, keyword and description metatags are information inserted into the header area of your blog that provide search engines additional data about the nature of your blog. While HTML code is not complicated, it still can be intimidating to the novice. Make sure that your blog platform has the ability to show you how to easily create these metatags; otherwise, you may need the services of someone with technical savvy.

Permalink

Every blog post has its own URL, which is its own permanent location on the Web. This URL is considered its "address." This is called a *permalink*. What that means is that the blog software creates a unique page for each and every blog post. This is how other bloggers are able to link to a specific post. From a search engine standpoint, because each post is its own page, it can be indexed individually by the search engines and catalogued. This is of inestimable value if you update your blog routinely and write about the same topics over and over. You begin to build a constantly growing "portfolio" of pages that over time will garner great search engine benefit. As an example, a post on Ralph Robert's "Flipping Frenzy" blog (www.flippingfrenzy.com/serendipity) on the topic of "real estate fraud" has as its permanent Web site address http://flippingfrenzy.com/serendipity/index.php?/archives/670-have-I-been-affected-by-real-estate-fraud.html. This is good search engine language for searches for *real estate fraud.*

BLOG POST CONTENT

More important than anything else mentioned so far in this chapter is the blog post itself. Two items are to be considered: what is said and how it is said. It is wise to stay on topic. While an occasional rant about some non-related issue might be of value, for the most part, focus your conversation around the central topic(s) of the blog. One tool to help with this is a *content calendar*. In the magazine publishing industry, this is called an *editorial calendar*. Whatever term is used to describe it, this calendar is a reminder to write about and include keywords organized by specific topic-related categories on a scheduled basis. This helps you to make sure that you don't get pigeonholed into writing about too few topics while overlooking other important areas that may be of interest to your visitors.

Keywords

Enhance your content with those all-important keywords. We recommend using a given keyword once in the title and then once or twice again in the post body to enhance its value to the engines. Don't overuse keywords, though, because you'll be accused of "keyword stuffing" and possibly be penalized by the very engines you are trying to attract. Create a list of 10 to 15 prime keywords to be used on a rotating basis throughout your blog. You also can have another list of 10 to 15 secondary keywords to be used less often but that will provide you with more search engine coverage. If you've done any Google Adwords advertising or employed an SEO firm to do optimization and search engine marketing for you, most likely you already have a long list of keywords available.

Length of Posts

How long should your posts be? We recommend anywhere from 150 to 300 words. Other experts have suggested 250 words as an average. This gives Google enough content to determine relevance based on topic and keywords. This is not to suggest that each and every post has to be this long. There are other factors to consider, such as reader attention span and the topic or genre being written about. Some posts may be only a paragraph or two. However, for the benefit of the search engines, it's best to make your posts longer.

Categories

Most blog platforms give you the ability to organize and archive your content by categories. We recommend that you select a blogging platform that permits categories because categories are valuable to search engines and will produce better results. Google recognizes categories, and by assigning a given post to multiple categories, you increase the chances of it getting higher rankings in Google. Having said this, however, we recommend that you don't be cavalier in naming your categories. Refrain from using fanciful terminology. Use practical, keyword-oriented terms. Think of what words your readers might be searching on and use those.

Frequency of Posts

When it comes to frequency, update your site as often as you would like people to visit, that is, daily, more than once a day, weekly, etc. The same holds true for search engines. How often do you want the Googlebot to come calling? The more frequently you update your blog, the more reason there is for Google and the others to index it. You want to give search engines as much reason to index your site as possible. Do you want to post three times per week, once per day, three times per day? Determine a posting quota. The more frequent the better, especially if you are using the blog for search engine positioning purposes. Plus, more frequent posting gives other blogs and Web sites more material to comment on, link to, etc. (You need all the "Google juice" you can get!)

Think of the search engine algorithm as the program logic that helps the search engine *spider* (a program that crawls through the Web in search of fresh content) determine how often it should visit your blog. You can improve your chances for good rankings simply by publishing more content more often! Because each new post gets its own page in your blog as fresh content is added, the overall number of Web pages increases. Google and other search engines tend to favor larger sites over smaller ones. Therefore, larger sites will tend to achieve better search engine rankings.

The benefits don't stop there. The greater the frequency of blog posts being added to a Web site, the more often search engine spiders will visit. Regular and frequent reindexing tends to raise a site's rankings in the search engines. Google almost certainly provides a boost to frequently and freshly updated sites.

BLOG-SPECIFIC SEARCH ENGINES

Without question, when it comes to search engines, Google is king. Latest reports indicate that Google is responsible for more than 42 percent of U.S. searches (ComScore Networks, February 2006). Not only is it the most popular search engine, but even the name has made its way into popular nomenclature; instead of searching for something, we "google" it!

However, there is no reason to underestimate the importance of appealing to Yahoo! or any of the other search engines. It is simply to suggest that getting "Google juice" is of the greatest value. In addition, Google now has a blog-specific search engine that is growing in importance and traffic (http://blogsearch.google.com).

Robin Good's "Top 55" list gives us an idea of how many search engines and directories populate the Internet (www.masternewmedia. org/rss/top55). This site contains a listing of over 160 such entities at the time of this writing. It is called the "Top 55" list because that is the number of compilers the list started with. It continues to grow. Most of these are blog-specific and contain such sites as BlogPulse, Feedster, IceRocket, and Technorati.

EXPERT'S TIP ➤ Register Your Blog

As soon as your site is built, register it with the following top search engines and directories:

> *Yahoo Directory:* https://ecom.yahoo.com/dir/submit/intro/
> *DMOZ:* www.dmoz.org/add.html
> *Technorati* (and "claim" your blog on Technorati): www.techno rati.com
> *BlogPulse:* www.blogpulse.com
> *Blogarama:* www.blogarama.com

(A more detailed list appears in Appendix D.)

A *Web directory* is a directory that specializes in linking to other Web sites and categorizing those links. Web directories often allow site owners to submit their own sites for inclusion in their directories. Some directories have editors who review the submissions to see whether the categories are correct. Web directory links are just as valuable as—and sometimes more valuable than—links from other bloggers. Directories help with PageRank and can get your site indexed by the search engines quicker, as the best directories are considered trustworthy links by the search engines.

PINGING

One final piece of advice: Include in your blog marketing what's known as *pinging*. By using a service such as Ping-O-Matic (www.pingomatic.com) or PingGoat (www.pingoat.com), you notify Web sites that keep track of blogs and publish content from them that your site has fresh content and to come index it. These are services that scan blogs regularly for updates and publish the most recent information. Letting such a service know that you have updated your blog is understandably important. To accomplish this, you send a *ping* to the service. These services then crawl and index your site, publishing your content and thus increasing your blog's popularity. Figure 2-9 shows you the Pingomatic.com index page, which con-

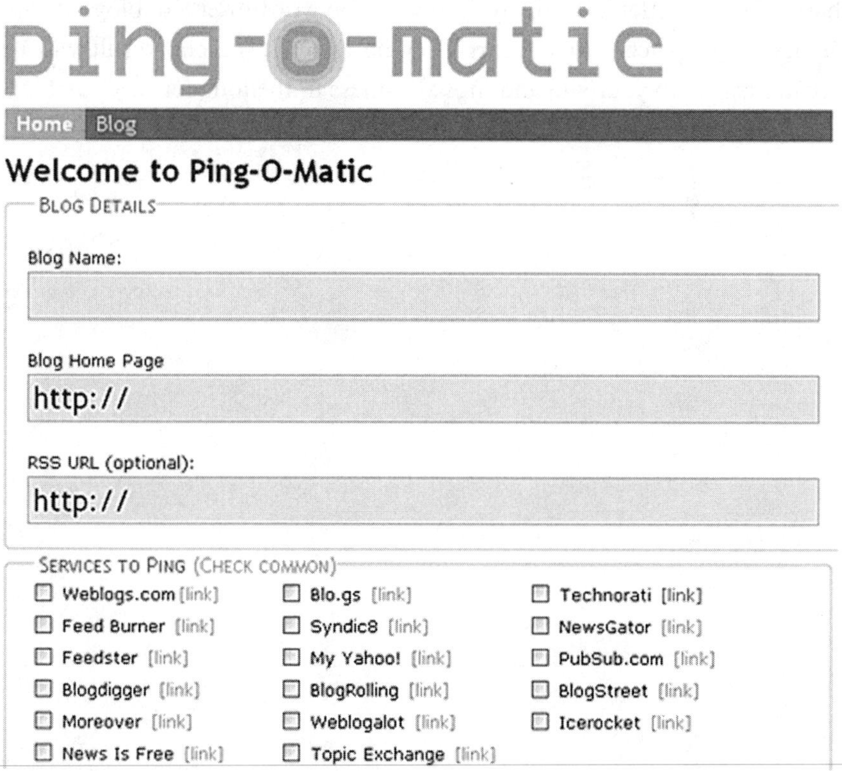

Figure 2-9. Pingomatic index page.

tains a list of Web sites it pings when you submit a particular blog name and URL.

This is not something that necessarily has to be done manually either, although it can be. Most blog platforms, particularly WordPress and Movable Type, provide places in the administrative interface for you to put URLs for Ping-O-Matic and others. Then, each time you update your site, a ping is sent automatically, and the applicable services, such as those listed in the screen shot in Figure 2-9 now have your fresh, new content in their results.

CONCLUSION

It's not just happenstance that blogs rank so well with search engines. There is a "method to the madness" that almost guarantees that if you have a well-written, routinely updated, keyword-oriented blog, it will achieve high placement in search engine results. The end result will be greater traffic to your site and more business in the long term.

3

Direct Communication

In the future, agents who want to maintain their competitive edge will need to . . . enhance their communication with clients through the use of the latest Web trends such as blogs.
                                    —California Association of Realtors
                                     2006–2007 Report
                                     "Internet vs. Traditional Buyer"

We have always held the opinion that people don't want to do business with businesses so much as they want to do business with people— particularly people they know and like. Paul grew up in a small town where everyone knew most everyone else, including the business owners. Gas was purchased either at "Doc" McCormick's service station or at Stampers just down the street. Groceries were bought at "Newt" McCormick's grocery store (Newt was Doc's older brother) and sundries at Guyses. There was one bank in town with two tellers, Frances and Linda. A single furniture store, Troy Brand Furniture, completed the downtown business sector.

The point we are making is that everyone in the town knew the business owners very well. Not only that, Paul's family knew their families. Their children went to the same schools, and all the families attended Sunday services together. Growing up in a small town had its advantages as far as knowing who you were doing business with and their reputation for being reliable and honest.

Things have changed. Often we don't even know our next-door neighbors, much less the person who owns the supermarket down the street. Most likely it's a far less personal chain outfit anyway. In this age of self-service megastores and nonpersonal online shopping, blogs can be an integral part of keeping you connected with your community. They can connect us and aid us in getting to know one another and building relationships with clients and prospects that can't really be done any other way online.

Toby Bloomberg, a marketing consultant and blogger in Atlanta, uses the metaphor of the old-time corner grocery store as a picture of how blogs help us to connect with one another. Here's her story in her own words:

> When I was a little girl growing up in Boston, I use to love going grocery shopping with my grandma. We would visit the green-grocer, the butcher, the fishmonger and my favorite, the baker.
>
> They knew my grandma well. And why wouldn't they? She had been shopping with them for many years. They knew she had five children and grandchildren she adored. They knew family dinners at Ida Marder's home meant lots of food and that meant lots of purchases.
>
> Grandma wanted only the best and sometimes "special," which was better than best! So the green-grocer would often put aside produce or the butcher would save a cut of beef or a chicken for her. If Grandma didn't think the chicken was up to her standard, . . . she was not shy about letting the butcher know it was not acceptable. And then advising him what to do about it. "Next time don't get one so old."
>
> When we went to the bakery, the lady behind the high counter would reach over and give me a cookie. Always. My, did I feel special! And I was special in her eyes. I was the granddaughter of one of her customers. She knew that if I was happy, then Grandma was happy. Even if Grandma's favorites weren't readily available, she wasn't going to the baker down the street. She was "brand loyal."
>
> And Grandma knew them too. She knew their simches (joys) and their tsoris (sorrows). If I were to say to Grandma, "You must have a pretty good relationship with the butcher to know about his daughter's operation." She would have said to me, "What relationship? They talk and I listen."

So it was. Customers and grocers both talked and listened. Customers and grocers both learned from each other what was important in their lives and in their communities. Customers and grocers both cared.

BLOGS CREATE RELATIONSHIPS

Blogging helps to recreate some of that small-town sense of community. How? By letting your clients and prospects in on your personality and human nature of the people who make up your company. Business technology guru Dave Taylor (www.intuitive.com) says that this is the "intersection of real estate and blogs." "Blogs let Realtors become people. I don't want to work with a national brand; I want to work with Jan Smith, my local agent."

Blogs allow clients and prospects to participate with you in the process of doing business. They do this by encouraging conversations. People don't want to be talked at, which is often the way marketing messages come across—*they want to be talked with*. Blogs allow this to happen.

"It's become an expectation that if you have a business, you have a blog," says John Jantsch, a Kansas City small-business marketing guru (www.ducttapemarketing.com/weblog.php). "Consumers are looking to find a community around your service. They're looking to have conversations with you about the products they're using."

According to Todd Carpenter, who blogs at Lenderama (http://blog.mariah.com), an industry blog for mortgage professionals, "Blogging provides an additional way to touch prospective and existing customers on a regular basis. It gives your clients a reason to return to your Web site, informs them on the latest tools at your disposal, and gives them the knowledge they desire to become an informed consumer."

The fundamental issue is to determine how you can communicate most effectively with consumers, not only to get search engine attention, but to make contacts and connections and become an influencer of opinion. Bloggers are "influencers influencing other influencers." This chapter focuses on ways to make your influence count!

BLOGS: PERSONALIZATION SUPERCHARGED

First, we need to establish the benchmarks, which are the general pillars of blogging tradition. They are honesty, transparency, and passion.

Blogging is at its heart an exercise in openness. One of the early definitions of a *blog* was "an online journal or diary." It is within the pages of a diary that you write your innermost thoughts and feelings. While we don't advise doing exactly that on a business blog, the spirit in which you write is the same. We call blogging "speak from the heart" writing. Because blogging is meant to be extemporaneous, blogs usually reflect a natural, genuine, and authentic tone.

Blogging is all about being real. The best way to be read is by keeping it real. Be yourself. Be honest. Let people see for themselves that you're just like that old-time grocer. Blogging is a place where you can share your professional experience, expertise, and knowledge, not in a self-congratulatory way, but as a mentor or teacher. It is a place where others can come to learn from you—not to be "sold."

Public relations blogger Jeremy Pepper wrote the following disclaimer on his blog entitled "POP! PR Jots" (http://pop-pr.blogspot.com). We think that you will find it to be very "real."

> *This blog belongs to me. All opinions and comments are fully my own opinions and comments, belong to me, and in no way reflect my employer's viewpoints or opinions.*
>
> *This blog is written under my own point-of-view, and I have full editorial control over its contents.*
>
> *When I correct mistakes—if they are beyond spelling and grammar mistakes—I will note that a post has been updated.*
>
> *I will be as transparent as possible, and if I do ever write about past or current clients—which will likely be never—I will fully disclose such activities.*
>
> *When I write here, I will try to set an example to clients, colleagues and other bloggers—PR or otherwise—on what I view as best blogging practices. PR and blogging need leaders, not sycophants and suck-ups. You will not see me link to link to get link-love.*

You might consider Pepper's "rules for blogging" as a template to follow in how you approach your own writing. Isn't it clear from these promises that Pepper is communicating to his readers that he is passionate about his writing? To blog regularly and in a way that connects with readers, you have to be passionate about your subject. If you enjoy your work as a Realtor and feel passionate about it, your enthusiasm will come across as genuine and will be well received by your audience.

Inject Your Personality

There is nothing worse than reading a boring blog. Be yourself. Inject your personality into the writing. Do you have a quirky sense of humor? Let it show through on the blog. Are you strongly opinionated? If so, let that be evidenced in your writing style. Figure 3-1 is part of a post from Rain City Guide's Dustin Luther (www.raincityguide.com) addressing the topic of whether to include home listings in a blog. Luther is responding to another blogger who believes that including home listings should be the focus of a blog and who isn't "terribly concerned with generating a loyal readership." Dustin makes his opinion *very* clear and takes a strong position on the topic, and for this type of writing he is considered one of real estate's most respected bloggers.

Find Your Voice

It's important that you find a style of writing that best fits who you really are. It's not unlike trying on a suit of clothes. How many times have you gone shopping for that business or casual outfit only to try on several before you find the one that best suits you?

According to Jonathan Miller, author of the well-known Matrix blog (http://matrix.millersamuel.com), "The hardest thing about a blog is finding its voice and sticking with it. The first couple of days that I posted, I was very sarcastic because that is how a lot of real estate blogs are. That has its place, but it was not what I was comfortable with, so I went back and ripped them all down and started over again."

Like Miller, you may have to experiment with different approaches until you find the one that is most comfortable. One way you'll know when you've found it is by the responses you receive. When you are yourself, writing with your "voice," people will respond.

However, I suspect that the author (who consults as an internet marketing expert) is under the assumption that because the home listing is in a "blog", there is some type of search engine optimization benefit over a standard website. Not only that, but I've heard this logic said enough that I suspect this notion is prevalent in the real estate community (i.e. blogs show up better than websites in search results!). **But this is a myth.** Search engines do not even try to tell the difference between a blog and a typical website (after all, they both just appear to be a collection of HTML code to a search engine).

The REASON blogs tend to perform better in search engine results than typical webpages is a direct result of the community that has created them. When done right, a community of bloggers share links with each other and not just any links, but deep links associated with quality content. To create a blog without the intention of creating community (or loyal readers for that matter) is to completely misunderstand the marketing potential of blogs.

I also believe the authenticity of the author when he says that he has had success marketing homes through his blog. However, I think the success has a lot more to do with the fact that the author *has created a community* around providing interesting advice for buyers despite his lack of care for these readers. When I said it was a mistake to put listing information on a blog, this is because there are better ways to display listings than in a blog post and too much self-promotion inhibits creating a community.

I actually remember noticing, and then unsubscribing, to the author's blog a long time ago because of all the self-promotional stuff. Interestingly, I would never have even found out about his post or linked to him had he not linked to me! By linking to me and taking part in the larger real estate blogging community, he has earned some backlinks to his site that will help him score better in search engines! A blog without community is simply a website that is organized chronologically and will be treated as such by the search engines.

If you want to see this bad idea taken a step further, check Ubertor's latest product where they sell a self-updating blog of featured listings. What could possibly be the benefit of a blog (with all it's ugly formatting restrictions) if it is self-updating? If an agent doesn't think it is worth their time to select a few featured listings for their blog, do they really think it will be worth anyone's time to read it? Let alone comment and link to these posts? Sometimes understanding whether or not an idea is a good marketing strategy takes little more than common sense.

Figure 3-1. Post from Rain City Guide blog.

Write Informally and Conversationally

You're not writing a formal article or essay. As we noted earlier, a well-written blog is "an e-mail to everyone." You're speaking from your heart as much as your head and often convey emotion as much as reason. To one degree or another, this is exactly how a blog post should be written—as if you are writing to a friend. Susannah Gardner writes in *Buzz Marketing with Blogs for Dummies,* "Try to write the way you speak." She suggests that it might be helpful to speak your entry out loud before trying to type it. (Of course, this type of approach requires that you write in the first person.)

Read and Learn from Other Bloggers

Business technology expert Dave Taylor suggests that one of the best ways to learn your blogging voice is to "read a lot of other bloggers and see if you're comfortable with their writing style, whether they seem to be a friend chatting with you or some self-important pontificating individual, and choose which you find most appealing." By reading other bloggers and getting a sense of what manner of writing resonates with you personally, you will be able to choose the most appropriate *blog style* for yourself.

Identify Your Audience

Who are you targeting with your blog? Is it the luxury real estate market, condo owners, vacation home buyers, suburban or urban, young or old, a particular ethnic group? Once you have a sense of the demographic, can you boil it down to one person? If so, pretend that you are writing to that person. Let your writing style and your content be what would appeal to and best resonate with that particular person.

BLOG WRITING TIPS

Just as with any writing you do, whether it is for brochures, press releases, or business e-mail, the specific writing of your blog will affect how you are perceived. In order to be viewed as a professional, we suggest that you use the following guidelines.

Check Your Spelling

While we do believe that blogs should be written in an informal style, if you are writing for business purposes, pay attention to spelling. Fortunately, most blog platforms now come with a spell-check function, so it's easy to do. If your blog platform doesn't include a spell checker, use the one built into the Google Toolbar. Another option is to create your post in a word-processing program and then copy and paste.

Use Proper Grammar

The use of proper grammar is a necessity for a business blog. This does not mean that you are forbidden to use colloquialisms or occasional forays into the use of poor grammar for effect. Ordinarily, though, it is in your best interest to be as grammatically correct as possible. Readers will form an opinion about you from the way you write; if you write in a professional manner, they will conclude that you conduct your business in a similar fashion.

Format Layout in a Clear Manner

Although this has little to do with finding your voice, text layout and alignment also need to be mentioned. Unlike print, there is no need to put two spaces between sentences. We don't live in the age of the Royal typewriter, and readers appreciate brevity. One space will do. Also, left-align each paragraph, and put a double break between paragraphs. It makes the page on screen much more readable. Use a font size that everyone can read. Many bloggers are Internet generation 20-somethings and can read small text, but many of your readers will be older and shouldn't have to strain to read your content. A font size of 10 to 12 points should meet everyone's needs.

Write Original Material

It would be very easy to just copy and paste what others have written and then write a comment or two of your own. However, doing so doesn't really tell the reader who you are, what you know, and what you believe. We suggest that at least occasionally you write a thoroughly original post. It is harder to do, but writing original content is one of the best ways we know to communicate your personal perspective.

In the book, *The Leadership Challenge,* by James M. Kouzes and Barry Z. Posner, Jossey-Bass, 2003), one of the chapters is entitled, "Find Your Voice." Although the book is directed toward leadership, the following excerpt sounds like it was written for bloggers:

Finding your voice is absolutely critical to becoming an authentic leader. If you can't find your voice, you'll end up with a vocabulary that belongs to someone else, mouthing words that were written by some speechwriter, or mimicking the language of some other leader who's nothing like you at all.

To become a credible leader, first you have to comprehend fully the values, beliefs, and assumptions that drive you. You have to freely and honestly choose the principles you will use to guide your actions. Before you can clearly communicate your message, you must be clear about the message you want to deliver. And before you do what you say, you must be sure that you mean what you say.

You can't believe in the messenger if you don't know what the messenger believes.

If you want to be a sphere of influence in your community and draw attention to your level of expertise and professionalism in your market, you must write your blog with a sense of assurance in your ideas and knowledge of your market.

In this way, your blog "voice" will resonate with your local community, and this direct communication will provide fruits for years to come. Ralph Roberts, *Time Magazine*'s "best-selling Realtor in America," puts it best when he says:

The best blogs are those with original and natural content. Just feeding in news sources isn't real writing; I think you've got to find your own information and put it out there. This is the right way to communicate directly with your community, your past customers and prospects. It's branding yourself, and it sets you apart. By spending just a few minutes a day writing to my community, I get comments and messages back from readers all day long.

BLOG POST FORMATS

Blogger extraordinaire Amy Gahran (www.contentious.com) suggests seven posting formats to enhance direct communication—particularly regarding the delivery of certain types of content. Her list follows, with comments we've added relative to real estate blogging.

Link-Only

Using this format, the blogger posts only a link or a group of links to another blog or Web site along with a few words of commentary. When blogging was in its formative years, link-only posts were common. Real estate blogger Hanan Levin's "Grow-a-Brain" blog uses this format extensively, but he is clever enough to add small nuggets that make you want to read more about what he has posted. These nuggets also reveal his sense of humor and irony and, in our case, made us want to meet him. Figure 3-2 is a sample post from Hanan's site.

Link-Blurb

This is similar to the link-only format with the exception that the added commentary is longer than a sentence or two. Often it is used to explain the value of the link in question. Jim Duncan's central Virginia real estate blog (www.realcentralva.com) often reflects this format. Here's a sample in Figure 3-3.

It's easy to imagine creating these link lists or blurbs that are relevant to your local community and that your readers will come to expect from you on a regular basis. This creates a blog that is "sticky," that is, one that

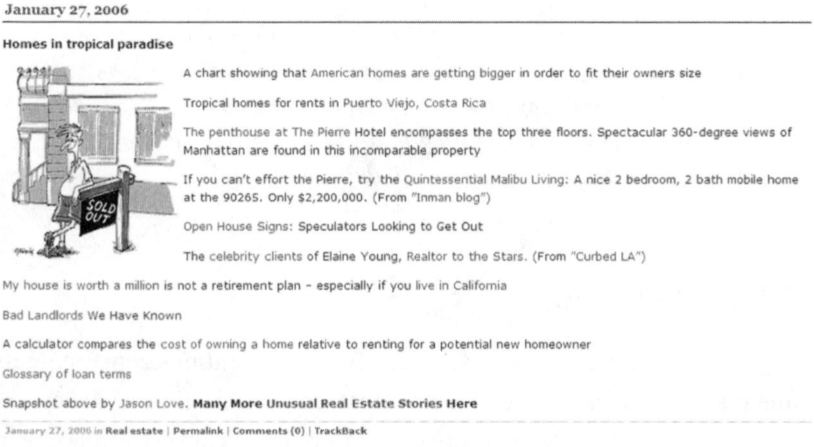

January 27, 2006

Homes in tropical paradise

A chart showing that American homes are getting bigger in order to fit their owners size

Tropical homes for rents in Puerto Viejo, Costa Rica

The penthouse at The Pierre Hotel encompasses the top three floors. Spectacular 360-degree views of Manhattan are found in this incomparable property

If you can't effort the Pierre, try the Quintessential Malibu Living: A nice 2 bedroom, 2 bath mobile home at the 90265. Only $2,200,000. (From "Inman blog")

Open House Signs: Speculators Looking to Get Out

The celebrity clients of Elaine Young, Realtor to the Stars. (From "Curbed LA")

My house is worth a million is not a retirement plan – especially if you live in California

Bad Landlords We Have Known

A calculator compares the cost of owning a home relative to renting for a potential new homeowner

Glossary of loan terms

Snapshot above by Jason Love. **Many More Unusual Real Estate Stories Here**

January 27, 2006 in **Real estate** | Permalink | Comments (0) | TrackBack

Figure 3-2. Post from Hanan Levin's Grow-a-Brain blog.

Links 04-13-2006

By Jim

The real estate blogosphere celebrates one of its own stepping to a new level. This is a testament to bloggers' influence, acceptance and the simple fact that Dustin is an innovator and leader. Here's hoping that move.com listens to him, lest they be left in the dust by the competition (pun intended).

Like it or not, Microsoft leads the way, not by innovation, but by volume. Those who have adopted RSS already - get ready for others to "discover" this technology.

> Live.com will be the first feed syndication experience for hundreds of millions of users who would love to add more content to their page, connect with friends, and take control of the flow of information in ways geeks have for years.

Do you know SEER 13 from SEER 10? After much discussion and court-time, the DOE upgraded the standard for air conditioning units, effective January 2006. Apparently, any existing units in stock may be used, but all new units must meet the new standard. This is good news for those seeking lower energy costs and higher efficiency, especially because "88% of homeowners say lower energy costs are "very important" when choosing an air conditioner."

MLS consolidation is necessary. Currently I am a member of and about to be a member of the Charlottesville-area MLS, Northern-VA MLS, Staunton/Augusta (Waynesboro!) MLS. The major impediments (over-simplified analysis) are: money, rule variations and turf.

I was at a home inspection this morning. While there, two of the Residents rode their bikes to the Medical School. That they didn't drive is a great thing.

1000 Barrels a Second may be the next book I read.

Technorati Tags: blogs, green, real estate, realtor, RSS, technology

Figure 3-3.   Post from Jim Duncan's real estate blog.

visitors will come back to again and again. The next time they have a real estate need, whose name have they seen over and over again as a result of your blog having become their local information source? Yours!

Brief Remark

The brief remark is a blog posting that generally is just one to three short paragraphs long. It can contain virtually any kind of content: an observation on current events, an idea, an event announcement, a question for readers, an anecdote, a joke, a description, etc. A good example of this type of blog is "The Real Estate Blog," written by Fran Vernon and Rowena Emmett. A sample is shown in Figure 3-4.

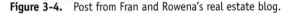

Sunday, March 12, 2006
The Best and the Worst Neighborhoods - by price appreciation

Forbes Magazine has listed the U.S. cities with the greatest and least amount of appreciation by zip code in the 20 largest metro areas.

At the top of the list? Chicago zip code 60602 with total price appreciation from 2003 to 2005 of 206.7%, followed by Miami and Dallas.

At the bottom? St. Louis, Missouri, followed by Phoenix and Chicago zip code 60611.

To read more: Best and Worst Neighborhoods

Permalink posted by The Real Estate Blog Author at 10:07 PM

Figure 3-4.   Post from Fran and Rowena's real estate blog.

List Format

A list-format blog posting combines several short items into a single post-ing. This could be a collection of anecdotes, examples, categories, links or link-blurbs, quotes, product recommendations, etc. It also might be a series of instructions for readers to follow. This format is useful when you want to do a "Ten Tips . . ." or "Five Reasons . . ." type of post. One of our favorite examples is Figure 3-5, the Rain City Guide blog (www.raincityguide.com) post by Dustin Luther entitled, "8 Common Mistakes Made by Real Estate Bloggers." (This could be a chapter all by itself!)

Short Article

This category includes any blog posting that runs from about 300 to 700 words. Typically, these blog entries are long enough to merit extending off

In putting together Rain City Guide with Anna, I think we've made every blogging mistake that is possible . . . [1]
In the spirit of learning from our mistakes, here are the top 8 mistakes that are made by real estate bloggers:

- Mistake #1: [2] Posting your listings. Treat your blog as a community resource and you will be rewarded. Treat it as an advertisement, and you will be unread.
- Mistake #2: Too much stuff on the front page (See photo on the right!). In a previous iteration of Rain City Guide I noticed that the site was slow because I was asking users to load too much stuff when all they really wanted was the content! I've cleaned up the interface and I feel much better about the site.
- Mistake #3: Create multiple blogs. Except for [3] Jonathan [4] Miller, I've never seen a good real estate blogger who could keep more than one blog interesting to read.
- Mistake #4: [5] Using a generic theme. Take the time to personalize the theme of your blog. Simple steps like adding your photo, editing the header graphic and changing around the colors can make a huge difference.
- Mistake #5: [6] Not reading other blogs. I built the original blog for Anna before I began reading other real estate blogs. No one ever linked to that site because I never linked to anyone else. [7] Unless you were one of the originals, you won't be able to get away with this and expect anyone to read your blog.
- Mistake #6: [8] Too much self-promotion. I stop reading blogs that include a paragraph about the author's exceptional services at the bottom of every post (especially if this paragraph is filled with links!). Again, [9] unless you were one of the originals, you can't get away with this and expect anyone to read your blog.
- Mistake #7: [10] Expecting people to comment just because you asked a question. If you want a response out of your readers, you really have to make it interesting. Before asking a question, make sure you're providing some content that is going to provoke them to respond!
- Mistake #8: Writing a post inspired by another blogger without linking to them. The temptation to keep readers on your site is great, but the benefits of [11] being a good linker are even greater!

As always, I'm interested in your feedback ☺ , and would be interested to hear if people could add two more so that we could come with a even ten.

Figure 3-5.   Post from Rain City Guide blog.

the home page to a separate full-text page but not so long as to require more than a few minutes of reading time. This differentiates short articles from brief-remark postings. Matt Lanning of "SFHomeBlog," a San Francisco real estate blog (www.mattlanning.com/blog.html), follows this style regularly.

Long Article

These are blog posts that extend beyond 700 words. They qualify as a true essay and are much more difficult to write, as well as to read. We don't recommend them unless you feel that you need to address a topic in depth. Because these tend to take on a less conversational tone, they need to be well written and well edited. In addition, unless your blog is intended as a public-policy forum, it should be written infrequently. Most blog readers are interested in capturing the message quickly, and long, involved posts have a tendency to be clicked away from.

Series Postings

A series of blog postings is an excellent way to approach almost any topic that is too long for a single post and can be divided easily into subtopics. A series is a collection of separate blog postings built around a theme that is posted over time.

In March 2005, David Smith, founder of the Affordable Housing Institute, wrote a series of posts on the future of New Orleans after Katrina. The commentary included an extensively researched analysis and quantitative projection of the city in terms of future population and housing. There was so much detail that it would not have been feasible for Smith to include all of it in one post. As such, the content was serialized into three segments entitled, "New, New Orleans: Diagnosis, Prognosis and Prescription" (www.affordablehousinginstitute.org/blogs/us/2006/03/future_quantifi.html).

In similar fashion, in 2004, during the time when blogging was just entering the business sector, Paul wrote a series of posts entitled, "The Future of Blogging in Their Own Words," which featured interviews with leading voices in the blogosphere at that time, such as Steve Rubel and

EXPERT'S TIP ➤ Blog Writing Suggestions

Here are some suggestions when it comes to blog writing:

Be careful about including press releases. It's okay to blog about them; just don't include them in a blog post. Press releases are too formal and stodgy to mesh with a blog.

Focus your content on your readers and not yourself. Because you're writing in a personal style concerning things about which you are passionate, it's easy to give in to personal interests. Keep your blog focused on your readers and their interests. It's okay to provide insight into your character and personality in ways that will make your blog inviting, relevant, and unique, but be sure to remember you are writing for your readers and not yourself.

Manifest your expertise on topics other than your company. Using your blog just to make you or your company look good is a definite turn-off. Experience teaches us to avoid this common error because you will likely come across sounding pompous and self-promoting. Figure 3-6 is an example from a blogger who understands this and is benefiting from it.

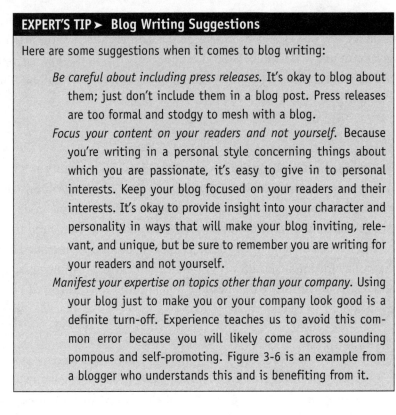

2. osman – **March 5, 2006**

Well done Dustin. This may be the best post yet.

On my blog I focus on being a resource for buyers and sellers and keep the self-promotion down to a minimum. Naturally, my listing focused site is linked on the blog and on the navbar. The way I look at it, when buyers in the Boulder Colorado are ready to look at property, I want to be there for them. In the meantime, there is a lot of research to do and I can help.

Since I live and breathe the market and have *some* analytical skills, I feel like I'm in a great position to add value for prospective clients. And with this strategy, in the few months I've been blogging, I've noticed an uptick in my regular website traffic as well as the blog.

It's turning into a nice win-win.

Figure 3-6. Comment left on Rain City Guide blog post.

Seth Godin, getting their take on what business blogging might look like in coming years. As you might expect, the commentary was too extensive for one post, so it was turned into a four-part series.

DETERMINE YOUR BLOG'S MISSION

Every successful blog requires well-defined and clearly stated purposes and/or mission statements—that is, reasons to exist. Susannah Gardner, in her excellent resource, *Buzz Marketing with Blogs for Dummies,* lists several possible mission statements to consider. Listed next are some of them, with comments we have added making them more relevant to real estate blogging.

Inform or Educate the Public

According to Gardner, providing timely information to readers is the most common purpose of a business blog. Realtor David Crockett's "Lake County Community Blog" (www.lakecountyblog.com) used this approach recently to advise the residents of Lake County, Ohio, of an upcoming presentation to their local Chamber of Commerce on economic development. The post is shown in Figure 3-7.

Encourage Dialogue with Current and Potential Customers

A blog can be used as a way for consumers to ask and get answers to questions. Adam Koval, a business consultant, started a San Francisco real estate blog, "SocketSite" (www.socketsite.com), in early 2005. Adam often found himself being asked about real estate because he had a financial background in investment banking. Adam's goal for "SocketSite" was to create a forum where he could share his own perspective on real estate issues and in addition build a community where others could share their views. Adam told us that he often writes posts in response to reader questions he's received in comments on his blog. "It's great to answer questions

Figure 3-7. Lake County Blog.

and provide a different perspective on what's really going on in real estate and what is happening in the market."

A blog also can be used as a way to generate feedback. Encourage participation by your local residents. Urge them to participate as a contributor to your online blog, and respond to your blog posts by leaving a comment. The way most blog platforms work is that when someone leaves a comment to a post, the writer of that post receives an e-mail with the comment and the e-mail address of the commenter. This is a great way to begin a dialogue with readers. As the author of the post you can then elect to add an additional comment, reply to the email, or both, as appropriate.

Convey a Sense of Company Personality and Culture

Blogs are a good way to make known what is special about your company's culture. Maybe your company is cool or a fun place to work. A blog is a good way to let people know this because it gives them an insider's view. One of the authors' clients has a category on his blog called "Inside the Company." The blog includes a post that shows a photo of the CEO sliding down the rail of an escalator at an airport as he was on his way to a trade show. That photo tells a story and gives readers insight into the CEO's personality ("He is a fun guy"). You open the gates to your company and, via the blog, let people walk inside.

It's not a matter of making people like your product or service. It's a matter of helping people to like *you* and to gain a greater sense of loyalty to you as a result. Using a blog in this way helps to create goodwill, which not only will result in revenue growth through the acquisition of new customers but will also strengthen the bond you have already developed with existing customers!

MONDAY, APRIL 03, 2006

▣ **Sarasota Real Estate News**

Sarasota, Bradenton, Venice on Best Cities list

Relocate America has included eight Florida cities in its 2006 list of the 100 best cities to live.

The list takes into account such factors as schools, economic health, population and crime rates.

Sarasota, Bradenton, Venice, Punta Gorda, St. Petersburg, Clearwater, Jupiter and Mount Dora all made the list. Manatee Chamber of Commerce President Bob Bartz thinks Bradenton's inclusion proves that it has been discovered, and he anticipates new development and redevelopment projects to emerge as a result.

Figure 3-8. Blog covering Sarasota, Florida.

Entertain Readers and Customers

A well-written blog is not only informative but entertaining as well. (See Figure 3-8.) Sarasota, Florida, Realtor Annette Ashley Smith uses her blog to target people interested in relocating to the popular resort/retirement community (www.sarasota-homes.blogspot.com). She blogs extensively about the community from her perspective as a resident and intertwines stories about life in Sarasota. Although she tries to make the blog informative, especially for someone interested in checking out the area, Smith keeps the tone light and fun to keep visitors coming back. Smith's blog allows her to interject her personality, and it becomes quickly apparent that she is an evangelist for the area.

Call to Action

In the United States, political blogs have been used to convince people to take specific action, whether it's to vote for a particular candidate or contact their congressperson about a hot issue. Business blogs also can be used as a "call to action." Your company produces a great service, right? Use a blog to help people find new and better ways to make use of it. You also might use the blog to provide incentives for people to help spread the message about your services, creating a viral effect. Figure 3-9 is an example of one of the authors' posts on "RealBlogging" (www.realblogging.com) calling on real estate bloggers to take advantage of the search engine benefits of links.

Be the Local News and Event Destination Site

Create an online local newspaper-like site that fosters a sense of community in your neighborhood. Invite local community members such as the Chamber of Commerce, charities such as the United Way, local school systems, kid and adult sports teams, businesses, and the people in your local neighborhoods to participate. Consumers are already turning away from mainstream media and turning to each other. Engage your local community to participate in this online community. The final result is a blog sponsored by you that is a destination site for the people in your community and those looking to move into your community. Because of the

Figure 3-9. Post on RealBlogging.com.

cross-posting that takes place among the bloggers, a sense of collaboration and participation arises.

Once again, when the participants and regular visitors to the site have a real estate need, who are they likely to call? Realtor David Crockett of The Crockett Team in Lake County, Ohio, established just this kind of community blog, the "Lake County Blog" (www.lakecountyblog.com). Here are some sample titles from recent posts:

1. "Pancakes for Pop—Father's Day Pancake Breakfast"
2. "Lake Metroparks Earth Day Coloring Contest"
3. "April Events at Lake Metroparks"
4. "The Great Western Reserve Clambake"
5. "Little Mountain Heritage Festival"

Did you notice anything interesting about these posts? There's not a word relative to real estate! In fact, in the first month that Crockett's site was in use, out of more than 200 posts, Crockett himself posted only five real estate—related posts. All the other content was created by community members. Shortly after the "Lake County Blog" went live, Crockett's local newspaper ran an article on the community blog entitled, "Lake County Enters the 'Blogosphere,' New Weblog Allows Organizations, Businesses Interactive Communication." The article went on to say:

> *An Internet-based community communications system, LakeCounty Blog.com, was unveiled Wednesday. It is meant to give area organizations an interactive forum with which to share information, garner feedback and provide access to their own Web sites. So if we're Lake County, and we want to get our message out and found by people, the better approach is "Let's all work together in one simple system in which we can all get our message out. It's like a constant living, breathing town hall meeting everybody can go to" [quoting David Crockett]. . . . The executive director of the Mentor Area Chamber of Commerce said she liked the idea of organizations working together to promote the county. "Any way you can bring to people to collaborate together, it's good for Lake County."*

This is a level of communication and collaboration with prospects, clients, and your neighborhood that can only be accomplished online through an active, vibrant community supported by blog technology. Static Web sites simply can't accomplish this. Blogging Systems, LLC's flagship product is devoted exclusively to creating community blogs (www .bloggingsystems.com) like this.

In fact, most companies combine several of these purposes into one blog. Don't feel as if you have to do everything at once, though. Start small and build from there. Multiple purposes are fine as long as there is an overriding central focus. To cover a topic that is totally outside the central focus of the blog, consider starting a separate blog.

CONCLUSION

One of the most important benefits of blogging is that it allows you to speak straight from your heart and mind—directly to the consumer in an honest and transparent manner. In so doing, you can establish yourself in an infinite variety of ways as *the* trusted advisor for real estate in your marketplace.

4

Brand Building

Blogging the Brand: . . . [C]orporations have figured out that tapping into the blogosphere is a great way to build relationships with customers. . . . [A]s the blog world has doubled in size every five months, companies are finding they can use its power to . . . build communities around their brands.

BusinessWeek, December 2005

How important is personal brand building in real estate? We've heard it said this way: Branding is more than just a business buzzword. It has become the crux of selling in the new economy. If the old marketing mantra was "Nothing happens until somebody sells something," the new philosophy could be "Nothing happens until somebody brands something."

Steven Van Yoder, author of *Get Slightly Famous,* says that brands have a number of strategic functions, enabling you to

- Differentiate yourself from your competition
- Position your focused message in the hearts and minds of your target customers
- Persist and be consistent in your marketing efforts
- Customize your services to reflect your personal brand
- Deliver your message clearly and quickly
- Project credibility

- Strike an emotional chord
- Create strong user loyalty

If you are not currently getting the results you want from your branding efforts, isn't it time to ask what can you do to change that? Blogs enable you to establish your brand as *the* trusted source for local real estate. In addition, blogs let you "tell the story" of your brand over and over again, allowing your customers to become both familiar and comfortable with it, something static Web sites can't do. Manifesting your brand with a blog allows for personalization, which is something that static Web sites can't do. Here's a comment from the "Blog Business Summit" blog (http://blogbusinesssummit.com) responding to the brand value of new-age real estate aggregator sites:

> *That's one thing about those [aggregator] Web sites that "sell" real estate services. When it comes down to it . . . there is no personality, experience and expertise in real estate behind all that html [computer code]. Blogging can relay those essential qualities of a real estate agent to the public.*

Greg Herder, CEO of Hobbs/Herder Advertising (an agency that specializes in real estate marketing), says that in most local markets there are far too many real estate agents for the average home buyer or seller to interview each one personally. Personal branding helps to simplify the consumers' choices, and the Internet is what consumers are now using to screen Realtors much more quickly. Herder's research shows that when faced with a large number of agents from which to choose, consumers select the agent who has the strongest personal brand presence in the area. Personal brand building is the cornerstone of a successful real estate career. Thus Realtors must create a brand to differentiate themselves from competitors in order to achieve that success.

The Internet has not helped matters either. In fact, it widens the circle of possible choices. Not only that, most agent sites on the Web make similar claims and promises as every other agent's site. So how can you build your personal brand and separate yourself from the competition? One sure-fire way is through a blog!

BUILD YOUR BRAND BY CREATING AN ONLINE PERSONA

One of the goals in creating a personal branding strategy is to achieve what's known as a *franchise in the mind.* When you think of soft drinks, what jingle comes to mind? In our day, it was "Things go better with Coke." How about insurance? Remember the slogan, "You're in good hands with Allstate"? How about buying books online? Do your fingers automatically start typing Amazon.com? And so it goes. These companies have spent billions achieving that *franchise in the mind.*

Suppose, if, in your local market, when people think of real estate, your name or your brokerage immediately comes to mind? Better yet, suppose you did not have to spend a fortune to do it? In today's information-overloaded market, personal brand building is more important than ever, and a blog is the most exciting and effective way to help you achieve this goal.

> ### EXPERT'S TIP ➤ Build Your Personal Brand
>
> Steven Van Yoder says, "In a crowded marketplace, where your potential clients and customers have lots of choices, you can stand out by being just slightly famous. It's not about being all things to all people, but being a minicelebrity to the right people. It's about targeting your market and developing a reputation as a great resource— trustworthy, knowledgeable, and close-at-hand.

So how do blogs help to achieve the goal of building a personal brand, creating that franchise in the mind, and becoming *the* real estate resource of record to those in your marketplace? Business technology expert Dave Taylor suggests that everything a Realtor does as a business that has a public face is de facto branding. In this respect, a blog is the same as a Web page, print brochure, or newspaper ad. What differentiates a blog, according to Taylor, is that it "gives you the opportunity to create a persona, a personality online."

Many agents have tried to build a personal brand on a single feature or benefit, such as experience, knowledge, education, or service. But it is hard to create strong emotional appeal by focusing on features and bene-fits. The best personal agent branding campaigns are built on the agent's personality, philosophy, or values. They are inherently emotional and, when used consistently, will give you a huge competitive advantage in the marketplace over time. For example, who comes to mind when you think of *Time Magazine*'s "Best Selling Realtor in America"? It's likely you would say Ralph Roberts. Figure 4-1 shows *personal branding* at its best!

Paul's son, Alan, is a waiter at a steakhouse. He has been waiting tables for a number of years and has learned a valuable lesson from which Realtors could benefit. You don't sell your product so much as you sell yourself. He knows that the more he injects his personality into interac-tions with customers, the more likely he is to walk away with a healthier tip and possibly even achieve some personal branding. Nowadays, it's not unusual for a customer to enter the restaurant and request his section.

Having a gregarious personality does not negate the need to provide good service or demonstrate expertise. Paul's son simply understands that knowledge without personality ends up with him walking away with less cash in his pockets and a lower rate of customer loyalty.

Most Realtors already know intuitively how important personal branding is. Photographs typically appear on everything from business

Figure 4-1.   Marketing slogan for Realtor Ralph Roberts.

cards to billboards to Web sites and yard signs. A blog will add not only another channel through which you can further personify marketing efforts but also a channel that will be more personal, more powerful, and therefore more effective in producing results! This is the true beauty of blogging. Not only does it allow you to demonstrate expertise or knowledge in certain areas, but it also allows you to express your personality. It allows the consumer to get to know you in a more personal way and create that all-important emotional bond.

Why is this important? As previously noted, home buyers and sellers really don't want to do business with a business; they want to do business with an individual—and preferably someone they know. Realtor Hanan Levin knows this. Levin's "Grow-a-Brain" blog is one of the most intelligent, entertaining, eclectic blogs in the blogosphere, and real estate is only a small part of his blog. He has over 100 categories! The site has served to bring him lots of business over the years. Levin's injection of personality, along with his ability to distinguish himself even among other real estate bloggers, has led to "Grow-a-Brain" becoming one of the most trafficked blogs on the Internet. The site has attracted over 4 million visitors, and that's only since it was redeveloped on a new platform two years ago.

Alex Stenback, author of the "Behind the Mortgage" blog (www.behindthemortgage.com), advises bloggers: "Let your personality come through. Don't use canned content, and don't regurgitate the same info as everyone else." He adds that it's also important to make blogs entertaining and he sees the element of humor as having value. Although he does not consider himself to be funny, apparently his readers do, and they come back to his blog to the tune of hundreds per day. He adds, "People who contact me to do business, thanks to the blog, contact me as if they already know me."

BUILD YOUR BRAND BY PROMOTING CONVERSATIONS

Blogging is about engaging in conversation. It facilitates a dialogue with the consumer. Why is this an important brand-building mechanism? Because it is through personal interaction that consumers get to know you. As they get to know you, they come to like you. Even better, they come to trust you.

How do blogs facilitate such conversations? One means is through a technology component built into the platform called *comments*. As discussed previously, when you write a blog post, readers have the ability to respond through the use of comments, and many blog platforms will send you e-mails containing the comments made by readers, along with their e-mail addresses. Some platforms send the e-mail with the reader's address in the From line. By simply hitting the Reply button, you have the ability to interact with that person one on one.

If the blog post is stimulating enough, it is likely to garner multiple comments. Figure 4-2 is from popular real estate technology blogger Dustin Luther in his "Rain City Guide" blog regarding a job change. Note the post footer-23 comments from loyal readers congratulating him on his new position.

While not all blog posts will spark this level of conversation, there are some specific steps that you can take to enhance your ability to use the inherent power of blogs.

Adding Some Sun to Rain City Guide   April 11, 2006

I'm extremely excited to announce that I've accepted a position with Move (HOMS) as the Director of Consumer Innovations.

Until recently, Move was known as HomeStore and they **(we!)** are the people who run Realtor.com, HomeBuilder.com, RentNet, Welcome Wagon, and a few other sites... The idea behind the Move brand is that we'll be creating a one-stop-shop for connecting consumers with comprehensive real estate information and expertise.

No surprise that this will be a huge change for me and my family. Not only are we moving to Southern California, but I will now have some actually time to spend pushing the boundaries of online real estate technology (I'm no longer a transportation engineer!?!). What a difference a year of blogging can make!

I imagine that there might be a question or two I could answer about this change, but I'll save the answers to what? why? how? and when? for future posts.

Find more articles tagged with:HomeStore, move, realtor.com, Site Info

23 comments | Author : Dustin

Figure 4-2.   Rain City Guide blog post.

Develop a Reader-Centric Point of View

Blogging in the early days was about conveying strong points of view. The emphasis was less on what the reader thought and more on what the blogger was sharing passionately of his or her own opinions and diatribes. Nowadays, things have changed. Bloggers are more of a commodity. There are plenty to choose from, and not unlike house hunting, readers can shop around until they find the best value. It is a buyer's market.

As such, without sacrificing passion and points of view, bloggers have to be very reader-focused in their writing. It may require a change of perspective on the very nature of blogging. Blogs never were intended as just a means for one-way communication but for stimulating dialogue between writer and reader. No longer can bloggers blather on and on without considering whether the information being provided has value from the reader's point of view. Your blog has to provide value if you expect readers to engage in conversation.

A truly successful blog formula consists of someone with something to say who is also attuned to what readers want to hear. If blogging is about creating and maintaining a conversation (and it is), it's best to stay focused on the interests of readers.

Participate in the "Grand" Conversation

Participate with other bloggers in your niche by leaving comments on their posts, as well as writing commentary about their posts. Link to them both inside your post and via trackbacks. This almost certainly will stimulate other bloggers to return the favor.

Ask for Reader Input

One of the best ways to get others to comment is to ask them to do so. Without a reminder, many readers won't naturally think of responding. Encouraging them to leave a comment simply by asking, "What do you think?" will be enough to get the conversation started. With sufficient coaching, you will find readers being more open to sharing their thoughts and viewpoints.

BUILD YOUR BRAND THROUGH
WORD-OF-MOUTH (WOM) MARKETING

Not only will consumers talk to you via your blog, they also will talk to one another. Your readers can become your best brand-building evangelists, helping you to spread your message and your presence throughout their networks. We call this *viral,* or *word-of-mouth* (WOM), marketing. Blogs are word of mouth-supercharged!

The best marketing that ever was, is, or ever will be is word of mouth. There is no dollar value you can assign to having someone else talk positively about you, your company, and your services. According to Paul Beelen (www.paulbeelen.com), an expert on technology's influence on advertising, marketing and media,

> *Hearing a positive comment about a product or service is still more powerful than many commercials or print ads, even more if that comment comes from someone you know and trust. The thing about word of mouth is that it typically stays within the cocktail party or the water cooler conversation. Until now. With millions of consumers also being publishers, this conversation is taken onto the World Wide Web, in the form of podcasts, wikis, forums and most importantly: blogs.*
>
> *Blogs allow comments, a feature that makes them actually just like conversations, available to the whole world. Also (and this is very important), they are search engine friendly, which means that services such as Google, Blogsearch and Technorati index them to convert them into a completely searchable database of cocktail party conversations. Instead of fake artificial commercial messages, people can now get real-life comments from peers on anything they want.*

According to a report issued by JupiterResearch of Darien, Connecticut, in October of 2005, "Companies overwhelmingly believe in the ability of consumers to influence one another's purchasing decisions." The research firm reported that 66 percent of the companies that participated in the survey believed that "the effect of consumer-created content on brands will greatly increase over the next 12 months."

Smart businesses will pay attention to blogs, using them as a kind of informal network of consumer opinion. Blogs have become a word-of-mouth marketing channel that allow companies to keep a pulse on their marketplace.

One way bloggers know that blogs initiate this kind of communication and opinion sharing is through tracking referral sources of click-throughs to their blogs. Using site-tracking statistic programs, which the better blogging platforms include, site owners are able to determine not only how many people are visiting the blog but also how they got to the site. One of the available statistics reveals when individuals click through to the site from a link within an e-mail message. This type of information tells bloggers that consumers are writing to each other and including a link to the blogger's site in the e-mail. Get enough of those, and you know that your blog has achieved WOM status.

For consumers, blogs are like customer reviews on Yahoo! Local (http://local.yahoo.com) or Amazon, which are helpful in making decisions about what to buy and whose services to use. According to a survey released by Yankelovich (a marketing firm based in Chapel Hill, North Carolina), one-third of all consumers would prefer to receive product information from friends and specialists rather than from advertising.

Steve Rubel, strategist for the PR firm Edelman, who maintains the popular "Micro Persuasion" blog (www.micropersuasion.com), argues that companies should embrace the in depth customer feedback that blogs offer. "It's a 24/7 focus group that's transparent and out in the open," said Rubel, adding that "the opportunity here is for companies to find their brand ambassadors."

Even if you are not associated with a well-known real estate brand or franchise, word of mouth can have a powerful effect for you individually. Agents, teams, and smaller brokerages need to learn strategic methods to create their "unique selling propositions" (USPs) so that they can effectively "walk with the giants," according to IMPREV founder and CEO Renwick Congdon, a well-known marketing and technology innovator. "Branding is no longer just something that's shoehorned into a marketing plan. It has become a core driver for successful businesses large and small," explains Congdon.

Integrating blogs into your mainstream marketing strategies is a successful branding technique for the small-business owner, according to a presentation Congdon made to the California Association of Realtors (CAR) at their Centennial Expo in September 2005:

> *Whatever the size of the organization, whether it's a single-agent enterprise or a corporation, they all share the same ambition-to be well respected and remembered as the obvious choice by their marketplace. Unfortunately, small businesses often feel overwhelmed by the big-budget efforts of their corporate counterparts and sometimes feel unable to compete on an equal plane. That's where understanding the strategy and tactics of successful branding and utilizing the technologies available to assist with this effort can make a tremendous difference in a small firm's ability to rise above the limitations of size and budget to compete on an equal footing with "the big guys" [RISMedia.com, September 15, 2005].*

Consider the following blog post from Forrester Research analyst Charlene Li, which includes kudos for the Realtor she used when purchasing a home:

> *We could not have gone through this process without our Realtor, Samia Morgan. I found Samia five years ago via Realtor.com—yup, I found her on the Internet. I was relocating to the Bay Area and wanted an agent who felt* very *comfortable using technology as a communication and marketing tool.*
>
> *While I had all of the latest tools at my disposal, I wouldn't have felt comfortable going into this complicated process without her. She was able to recommend a great house stager, builder, and even lent us a free truck to help with moving. But most importantly, she used her considerable connections and experience in the real estate market to understand how the market was changing—especially useful in a jittery market. We were extremely happy with both sides of the transaction, and especially the role that Samia played—we don't think we could have successfully navigated the process on our own, nor do we ever really want to in the future!*

Simply stated, you cannot buy this kind of marketing. We've said it before, but it's surely worth repeating: Blogs are word of mouth—supercharged!

BUILD YOUR BRAND THROUGH CONNECTIONS

One of the biggest advantages to using blogs is connecting in personally powerful ways with your target audience. By establishing deeper relationships, you are able to effectively influence how people think and feel about you and your business. Your connection is what will create your blog's greatest success. How do you make these vital connections? By being yourself, sharing what you know—your expertise and experience—and injecting some of your personality into the mix as well. You don't have to be a professional writer to accomplish this either. This is part of the fun of blogging; it doesn't require a degree in journalism. It does require honesty, transparency, and a heartfelt desire to share something that will benefit readers. If you can do this, you will connect!

BUILD YOUR BRAND BY CREATING COMMUNITIES

One of the more recent and most notable trends on the Internet has been the formation of affinity-based communities and social networks. Sites such as LinkedIn and MySpace allow individuals to coalesce around a given topic or issue of shared interest. Effective blog marketing has mirrored that trend with the creation of community blog networks—sites that tie individual blogs together under a single portal.

A community blog hosted by a Realtor, team, or real estate company has phenomenal potential to establish your blog as *the* place to go in your community to find out "what's happening!" A Realtor-sponsored community blog will include a whole series of individual blogs hosted by community members such as the local Chamber of Commerce, United Way, local city governments and school systems, newspapers, business journals, economic development groups, sports teams, etc.

The recent explosion in Web sites offering hyperlocal content (neighborhood and community news) supports the movement of Realtors into community blogging. Lots of media outlets cover what's happening across the world, nation, state, or even major metropolitan area. The problem is that people care most about what's happening in their own neighborhoods. Who better to take the offline community contacts they already have in their local neighborhoods and put them online than Realtors who are already tuned into the local community? The final result is a Web site sponsored by you, your team, or your brokerage that becomes a destination site for those interested in your community.

Community Blogs and Your Business

From a business standpoint, community blogs offer very special advantages. Realtors seeking to extend the value and reach of their brand can empower and engage staff, customers, visitors, and other constituents by offering them their own individual blog sites within the branded community.

A frequently overlooked benefit of a community blog is the enormous potential opportunity for you as the host of the community, whether you are a real estate agent or a real estate company, to establish and build on the relationships established with the hosts of the other blogs on your site! Most often the other blog hosts will be the movers and shakers in your community. These contacts are likely to be extraordinarily valuable.

"YoChicago" is one service trying to capitalize on this sense of community by including in the site property searches, neighborhood journals, guides, and other resources. "YoChicago is an attempt to go back to the basics of newspapers and start building a community around content," said Zekas, YoChicago's creator, according to an "Inman News" article from February 2006 (Inman.com, "Community Real Estate Sites Taking Off"). Zekas recruits hundreds of writers to provide content for online neighborhood journals in the seven counties around Chicago. "One thing that's been missing on the Internet is really hyperlocal kind of content," said Zekas. Volunteer writers supply much of the site's content.

Another approach to providing a community blog platform is one taken by Blogging Systems, LLC (www.bloggingsystems.com). Blogging

Systems' flagship product, Community Publisher, has been designed with real estate companies and real estate agents in mind, and enables both groups to create and extend marketplace brand awareness. This blog platform contains all of the functionality in a "ready to use-out of the box" format that enables total customization, which helps Realtors to create an online hyperlocal newspaper-like site that fosters a sense of community among the invited community bloggers such as the previously noted Chambers of Commerce, charities such as the United Way, local school systems, sports teams, etc., and the people of their local neighborhoods. Content is created by each community blogging member and aggregated into the main community site. A community calendar lists special events occurring in the community. The platform also includes the capacity for podcasting, video and more.

Community blog platforms are a unique marketing approach guaranteed to increase a company's visibility within the local community and create closer ties to it. The final result is a Web site sponsored by the local Realtor that becomes a destination site not only for your target market but also for outsiders seeking to learn more about your community.

BUILD YOUR BRAND COST-EFFECTIVELY

Hobbs/Herder, the real estate marketing firm mentioned earlier, suggests that for as long as you are in real estate, you need to invest at least 30 percent of your overall marketing budget in personal branding. Further, if you are new to the industry, the company suggests spending 75 percent of your budget on personal branding.

This is yet another reason that blogs are good brand-building tools—they are inexpensive to deploy. Depending on the blog platform chosen, you can spend as little as nothing. For example, Blogger.com is free. Just remember, you get what you pay for. As your knowledge of blogging and blog tools increases, you'll most likely find that few free solutions provide the ability to customize a blog with the degree of professionalism a top agent would require. (See the list of potential blog platforms in Appendix B.)

Community blogs offer Realtors the opportunity to choose the best of the best when it comes to blog platforms. While an interactive, fully

EXPERT'S TIP ➤ Use a Blog for Recruiting Purposes

Ask any broker/owner whether his or her only reason for advertising and other branding efforts is to generate new home buying and selling prospects, and every one will tell you that recruiting is another very important reason. Brokers are continuously seeking new recruits to replace those that have left the business or to increase market share. New licensees often select their brokerage affiliation based on the amount of advertising that company does. Just like buyers and sellers, potential recruits are persuaded by effective branding. For example, a real estate blog platform such as a Community Publisher site, that provides agents access to a blogging platform with all of the essential features of a sophisticated blog marketing tool, is being used more and more by leading real estate companies to establish themselves as *the* company of choice, not only for new agents, but agents seeking a new company affiliation.

functioning community blog platform is more expensive than a single-user site such as TypePad or Blogger, it is possible for Realtors to be able to generate local advertising revenue from the community blog—offsetting any associated costs.

Even if your marketing budget is small we suggest that a blog is the only Web presence that you may need. A blog can incorporate all the regular Web site features such as your business location, contact details, and services/product pages. However, the real power of a blog comes from all the extra advantages that are *not* available with a regular Web site; this can't be seen or appreciated until you actually implement and experience your own blog! Each and every one of those functions can be facilitated via your blog.

PARTNER WITH YOUR CUSTOMERS

Realtors have had at their fingertips an array of powerful tools to support development of a brand. Television and newspaper advertising, billboards, and direct mail are just a few. Consumers were the passive audience, taking in these messages and, hopefully, choosing to do business with the broker or agent who best attracted their attention. At the core of all this "branding" was control. Companies could, with a fair amount of success, control their brand message, ensuring that it resonated with consumers in the way they intended.

Today, things are changing. Marketers are losing control over their company's brand as consumers are gaining influence through the interactive channels of Web-based communications (newsgroups, blogs, etc.) The new communications channels—especially blogging—have wrestled control over the brand from the company. Postmodern branding, with its implications of distributed power, has emerged.

Smart companies now realize that their brand is capable of being enormously enhanced by their audience through the effective use of a blog, in addition to efforts by their resident "branding expert." The true "brand" of an organization will emerge from interactive market conversa-

---

EXPERT'S TIP ➤ Build a Partnership with Your Customers

As you think about using blogs for branding purposes, here are some points to guide you:

Be transparent and personal. Avoid formal or corporate-sounding language. Be open to self-disclosure, and don't talk down to your readers. Try to create a sense of inclusion, where you value their input as much as your own.

Speak clearly and with a high degree of relevancy. Make your communication plain, and don't be afraid to voice your opinion. Strong opinion is one of blogging's historic hallmarks. Articulate your point of view, and keep your comments topically relevant.

Speak passionately. Blogging is a marketing tool, but not an impersonal one. The best blogs are those where the author has obvious passion for the topic. Passion begets passion. Let yours show through, and others will catch your enthusiasm and pass it along.

tions among consumers. Smart companies will *embrace* this new reality and become partners with their customers in creating company brands.

Last year, the *New York Times* reported on a blog by Mike Kaltschnee in which he wrote about the movie rental company Netflix. "I post anything I find interesting, and it turns out 100,000 people a month find it interesting, too," said Kaltschnee. Of these noncompany brand-creating blogs, Ken Ross, a vice president of Netflix, said, "In addition to viewing blogs as another media channel, it allows us to keep our pulse on the marketplace." Said Jackie Huba, author of the book, *Creating Customer Evangelists,* "They felt like they own the brand, that it's theirs. They feel like they're doing the world a service" ("Brand Blogs Capture the Attention of Some Companies," *New York Times,* October 24, 2005).

CONCLUSION

We'll close this chapter with a quote from a blog post found on the "Small Business Branding" blog (http://smallbusinessbranding.typepad.com) entitled, "The Blog Is the Only Online Marketing Tool You Need." It states convincingly the power of blogs for branding purposes and while it focuses on small businesses the observations apply equally as well to any size organization.

> *I am now totally convinced, with thanks to blogging, that for small businesses there is no more powerful brand message to project than yourself. Even for big business, a personality brand can be a powerful message. "Richard Branson" is almost as meaningful as the Virgin brand itself. I think they are synonymous in a lot of ways. I see Virgin and I think Richard is behind this, so it's got to be good. If it wasn't for the corporate structure of big business, where ownership is not in the hands of one person and the "captain of the ship" changes regularly, I'd be a proponent of personality branding for big business too.*
>
> *Small business branding is not a good logo, a rhyming name, or special font. Small business branding is the owner. It's what the owner does, says and how the owner's traits come through in every aspect of the business. It's the way relationships are built and maintained, the way a person does business and treats other people. It's how rapport is established at an individual level, where trust and comfort exist as human characteristics, not from theme music, models or slogans.*

5

Competitive Differentiation

Blogging provides yet another tool to help real estate agents maintain an open dialogue with their clients and provide them with valuable information . . . by posting local current events.
—STEFAN SWANEPOEL
Swanepoel 2006–2007 Trends Report

What makes you or your brokerage different from your competitor down the street? How can you make a prospective customer understand that you have something better to offer? How can you sell the prospect on the benefits of choosing you over the competition? One way is to use a blog.

Blogs enable you to "tell the story" of your business over and over and over again. One of our favorite examples of a small business using a blog for this purpose is a custom sign maker in Lincoln, New Hampshire, the Lincoln Sign Company. It's a small business run by J. D. Iles, who uses a blog—www.SignsNeverSleep.com—to showcase his business. He was one of the first small businesses to employ a blog as a marketing tool, and after just a few minutes on his site, you'll catch on quickly as to how he differentiates himself from the competition. Here's how J. D. describes his site:

This Web site is a running commentary on what we do, day-to-day, to create terrific signs for your business or home. If you scroll down the page, you will see an online record of our daily routine. We update this page just about every day, so if you visit us from time to

time, you will be able to see all the different types of projects that we
work on, and you might even get to see your *sign in the process of*
being created!

The use of blogs in this fashion sets businesses apart from their competition. (We tell everyone that J. D. is a model small-business blogger who
is worthy of imitation.)

For Realtors, the goal of competitive differentiation is more difficult
to achieve than for a sign maker. The approach, however, is different
because even though you are dealing with tangibles, such as residential
homes or commercial properties, these are not really your products. In
your case, it's the intangibles that set you apart. Your knowledge of your
area or of the industry, your years of experience, your personality—these
are what differentiate you. Blogs enable you to manifest these attributes
and communicate them to your target market.

A blog is like a continual tour with you as the guide, so that visitors
can get to know you well. Blogs enable you to take your readers on a journey into who you are, what your business is all about, and what makes you
a more worthy candidate than your competitor. Here are three examples
of very successful real estate industry bloggers and why they find blogs
effective in separating them from their competition.

THREE EXAMPLES

Alex Stenback

Alex Stenback, a Minneapolis, Minnesota, mortgage banker and blogger,
puts great emphasis on geotargeting his blogging efforts. "I'm very focused on my local market in the Twin Cities. There are fewer people talking about mortgages locally via blogs, so I can stand out better than if I
were trying to cover issues at a national level," says Stenback. "You get a
much better chance of building readership when focused locally. You can
break stories and provide information people care about." He adds, "The
more local you get, the better off you are."

So popular is Stenback's blog that he makes this claim: "I own the
online conversation about real estate and mortgages so far as Twin Cities

is concerned. My blog makes finding information about these topics easy, as I aggregate news otherwise found in a variety of sources."

Stenback also advises Realtors to "stay true to yourself and don't be all things to all people." He suggests that Realtors take a position and don't worry about appearing controversial or offensive. "Taking a position on an issue of importance is certainly one way you can differentiate yourself from your competition."

Tony Kawaguchi

Hawaiian Realtor and blogger Tony Kawaguchi says that he started blogging (www.honolulu-realestate.net/blog.htm) as a way to be unique. "I googled the phrase 'unique marketing for real estate' or something to that effect and found that many of the sources I was reading were blogs," says Kawaguchi. "Then, I thought, no one is doing this in Hawaii." His initial thought was that blogging was a way to add more interesting content to his Web site. However, he began to realize that it was a way to help him establish credibility in the marketplace and make himself stand out. Although he has been blogging for only four months at the time of this writing, based on his experiences to date, he anticipates that his blog will contribute as much as one-third to his entire business revenue.

Noah Rosenblatt

New York City Realtor and author of the popular "Urban Digs" blog (www.urbandigs.com), Noah Rosenblatt says that it is his content that gives him a competitive edge. "I never try to sell myself or my services but rather focus the content, on educating New Yorkers." Never selling himself might be an understatement in Rosenblatt's case because he never lists exclusive properties for sale on his blog. "I do zero marketing for my own exclusives. My blog purpose is not to sell my properties but simply to educate New Yorkers, not to show them what I'm selling." Quite to the contrary, he often will list properties represented by other brokers.

One thing Rosenblatt does that he attests gives him a competitive edge is a daily two-hour live online chat. Participants interact with him through a chat feature that he includes as part of the blog template. Yet the chat, just like the blog content, is focused on educating consumers rather than self-promotion.

CREATE A VENDOR PORTAL

Small-business marketing expert John Jantsch says: "Real estate agents do well when they can put together a trusted army of all the things that home owners need when they buy and sell. Really ramp that theory up with a formal network of resources that blog with the agent as the hub, and you've got a powerful and useful differentiator."

Imagine having all the necessary real estate-related services within a single blog—a *vendor portal*—with you as the portal sponsor. The vendors each could blog about their services and offer discounts to home owners, buyers, and sellers, and with each offering, your branding would be part of the presentation. Most Realtors have already established relationships with every type of real estate-related vendor in their market. Bring them online with you and create a vendor-offering portal for them to reach your prospects and clients.

REVISITING THE COMMUNITY PORTAL

Jantsch also advises Realtors to think of a blog as a community portal, not a single blog but a network or "community" of blogs linked together through a single portal. He suggests offering them to schools, clubs, and sports teams, with associated branding logos and pictures that show you as the sponsor. Your role is to network with these groups and organizations, providing them with this new tool that enables them to broadcast their special events, announcements, and other news of interest to the community. Then who will they call when it comes time to sell? The friendly real estate agent that provides their school sports calendar and online blog!

When Is a Blog Not a Blog?
When It's a Community!

As noted previously, one Realtor who has done this very thing is David Crockett, a broker in Mentor, Ohio, a Cleveland suburb. His "Lake

COMMUNITY BLOGGERS

> Chambers of Commerce Blog
> City of Mentor Blog
> Concord Township Blog
> Geauga County Blog
> Ladies and Gentlemen Blog
> Lake Catholic High Blog
> Lake County Business Journal Blog
> Lake County Economic Development Blog
> Lake County Schools Blog
> Lake County Visitors Bureau Blog
> Lake Metroparks Blog
> Lakeland Community College Blog
> Leadership Lake County Blog
> NDCL Blog
> New Construction Blog
> Newell Creek Blog
> Real Estate Blog
> The Sports Blog
> United Way Blog
> Wines and Wineries Blog
> Daybreak Coffee Company
> What's Happening Blog
> Barnes & Noble (Mentor) Blog
> News Herald Blog
> Lake County History Center

Figure 5-1. Lake County Blog list of community bloggers.

County Blog" (LakeCountyBlog.com) has more than 20 such community entities participating on the site. He has minimal branding on the sidebar of the blog linking to his company and MLS Web sites. Figure 5-1 is a screenshot of the "Lake County Blog" community blogger list.

Following are some of Crockett's thoughts on using his community blog to differentiate himself from other Realtors in his region.

When I first heard about blogs, I was fascinated with the idea of the interaction among people. The problem I saw with blogging was that it was just another Web site in terms of working to get people to find it. It's hard enough to get people to your regular Web site with all the marketing you do. Here you have another Web site you have to drive traffic to. It may even be more difficult because it doesn't have house information on it, which is what people are looking for. It has conversations, and most people try to avoid talking to a Realtor, and they're not going to a Web site to find you. Plus, I don't want to type that much. If you have a blog, you have to add content all the time.

I saw blogs as a unique opportunity, but not the way it comes out of the box. So that's where the community blog idea came about. I wanted more people involved in doing the posting. Second, I'm pretty involved with my community. Our county is the smallest in Ohio, but it has a unique identity in itself.

Crockett's community blog enabled him to bring a benefit to his community that no other local Realtor did—an online interactive destination site for local news and information in which all the community members could participate. This "service" to the community and his member bloggers isn't something any other Realtor in his area was offering and has clearly enhanced Crockett's reputation as a real estate leader in his primary marketing area.

CREATE AN EXPERTS' BLOG CHANNEL

According to Jantsch, another way to use blogs to set yourself apart from your competition is to network with other specialists in real estate—related fields—mortgage bankers, home inspectors, and the like. Offer them a guest expert spot on your blog, or create one for them using the community portal idea mentioned earlier. "First off, if you do this, your blog would get a lot better and lot more active," says Jantsch, "but, and maybe more important, you also may cement a relationship with these other referral sources and publicly be seen as the hub of a powerful network."

A great example of this approach is the "Rain City Guide" blog targeting the Seattle, Washington, real estate market run by Dustin Luther. What started out as a way to help market his wife Anna's real estate business has turned into a cottage industry. It has become one of the leading real estate blogs not only in Seattle but also in the entire country.

Luther has assembled a team of 10 bloggers covering a variety of topics, including real estate technology, real estate law, mortgages, and area neighborhoods. "I was not seeing a lot of good information coming from agents, not on the Web at least," says Luther, "so I started blogging about stuff that interested me about real estate. Because of the work involved with blogging, we pulled together a community of bloggers. They contribute even when [we] don't have time to."

Luther said that he brought together contributors from the industry who could complement his area of expertise, real estate technology. "The other contributors write completely different entries that speak to completely different groups of people. . . . Rain City has become a conversation among real estate professionals." As a result, the site turned into an "online real estate newspaper" widely read by many in the Seattle area.

LISTING APPOINTMENTS

Imagine that you're on a listing appointment. You've got your flip chart, your Comparative Market Analysis (CMA), and all your regular tools. You go through your presentation, and at the end, the prospect says, "Thank you very much for your time, but frankly, we've heard the same thing from the other two agents we've interviewed." Chances are you've heard this many times. What else can you bring to your arsenal that isn't yet commonplace among your competition?

Ken Baris, president of West Orange, New Jersey-based Jordan Baris, Inc., Realtors, tells us, "Blogs!" Baris believes that neighborhood blogs, if done right, can be excellent tools for sales agents to promote their listings and distinguish themselves from other agents. He also pointed out to us that having a blog with enough worthwhile content can make the public feel like part of that online community. These features of blogs enable you to promote yourself to your listing prospects as different and better than the rest of the field when it comes to real estate marketing.

Baris does warn Realtors not to start blogging simply for the purpose of using blogs. He suggests that the blog needs to be "sticky" in order to cause readers to come back. The way to do this is by providing useful information.

NEW AGE FARMING

What is the single most unpleasant thing that new Realtors (and experienced ones, for that matter) complain about? If you said "farming," congratulations. Yet what is one of the most important things most real estate trainers say that real estate agents need to do on a regular basis? Right again—farming. But farming is hard. The old-school method requires walking about, knocking on doors, and making those dreaded cold calls. When you do knock on those doors or get through to someone on the phone those few times, can you really differentiate yourself? Can you truly explain why you would provide better service than other agents—with reasons that the other agents aren't themselves claiming?

Imagine if you didn't have to spend all that foot and phone time, all that time mailing and dropping off magnets and calendars. Wouldn't it be great if your farm could come to you instead of the other way around? Wouldn't it be great if there were some way your community residents could regularly visit you without your having to chase after them? Blogs enable this to happen. Here's more of what Realtor Tony Kawaguchi has to say about making himself stand out through his blog:

> There are so many different ways to advertise real estate now, and there's so much competition in every area. My blog is like a backdoor way of explaining the benefits of living in Hawaii or how to move here. Blogging about real estate is very specific. I provide information that eliminates the need for my readers to do their own research. Then, when they're ready to buy or sell, they'll see me as the expert.

Kawaguchi says his blog has resulted in

- New clients from New York and California
- Up to 50 blogsite visitors per day
- Meeting lots of industry participants online with reciprocal business taking place

- Great public relations, including two newspaper articles
- His blog being placed on numerous other blogger's blogrolls

These new clients from New York and California, the 50 visitors per day to Kawaguchi's blog, these prospects to his "online farm"—he didn't have to go out and get them; they came to him via his blog!

As a first mover or even as a follower who creates an outstanding blog with significant local readership, you can sell yourself as having a tool that most of your competitors don't have and one that many of them may not even know about. This is differentiation at its best.

Dewita Soeharjono, a Realtor in the greater Washington, DC, area, was looking for a way to differentiate herself from the competition. She said, "There are 11,000 Realtors in Virginia, and I wanted to find a way to set myself apart." Her answer is the "Urban Trekker" blog (http://metrodchomes.typepad.com). She chose to focus on life in urban areas and write about real estate trends in the DC market as well as nationally. The blog became a way for her to showcase her expertise and expose herself to a wider audience than would have been possible any other way. Her approach has proven to be worthwhile. Soeharjono says that as much as 25 percent of the business she receives has come as a direct result of her blogging efforts.

CONCLUSION

These Realtors, and many others like them whom we interviewed in preparation for writing this book, demonstrate one principle worth noting: Using a blog to focus on a local market is a highly effective way to give yourself a distinct competitive advantage!

6

Positioning Yourself as the Expert

Maintaining a blog can transform an ordinary, everyday person into a local, national, or even international expert in their field.
—WAYNE HURLBERT
Blog Business World

Thanks to technology, a big change is coming in the way real estate marketing is done that may well affect the role Realtors will play. The Internet has empowered consumers to research information, learn about housing trends, determine homes' values, and choose the homes they want to tour. A recent survey notes that more than 70 percent of home shoppers who come to real estate agents for assistance in buying a home already have relevant local home information from the Internet (California Association of Realtors, "Internet vs. Traditional Buyer," Real Estate Research Report, 2006-2007). Further key findings from the report include

- The typical home buyer is now an Internet user (70 percent use the Internet "as a significant part of the home-buying process").
- Buyers report that the Internet provides a greater sense of control over the home-buying process.
- Most buyers consider the Internet as an information resource rather than as a substitute for a real estate agent.

Figure 6-1. Redfin map of listings.

Redfin CEO Glenn Kelman says of this shift: "I don't see Realtors as going away, but they do have to make a change, especially in larger markets where competition is so intense. It's important to have online marketing skills such as search engine optimization, e-mail, and blogging (Figure 6-1)."

Business technology expert Dave Taylor says: "Realtors have been slow to adopt new technologies, and that's a mistake. They need to become technically savvy and should embrace its use."

He recommends that in order for Realtors to remain relevant in this technological age, they should distance themselves from being an information broker and become a community representative. Agents and brokers have specific knowledge about the community that can be used to demonstrate their value and expertise. Taylor suggests writing about neighborhoods, homes that are under- or overpriced, how to sell or buy a home, and colleagues with whom you work who provide exceptional service.

Mortgage blogging specialist Todd Carpenter says that the personal touch is still of prime importance. In his opinion, most people are not going to trust a home sale or purchase to data from a Web site. Carpenter thinks that Realtors need to worry less about technology solutions and focus more on having a presence that proves their worth and their value. He urges Realtors to use a blog to say to consumers, "Zillow doesn't know this neighborhood—I do; I can tell you what houses are really worth." Carpenter also notes that just because people are going to the Internet first for their home shopping doesn't mean that they are necessarily going to Realtor.com. "They could be going to Google first and finding you." The Internet can level the playing field in this way.

Dustin Luther of Rain City Guide agrees. "Google searchers won't show up at big data sites but at a newspaper article or at a blog or somewhere where someone has provided good context for the searcher's question in Google." He adds: "It doesn't have to be a blog. It can be a Web site. But blogging is so darned easy."

CASE STUDY: *Charlene Li*

Earlier this year, Forrester Research analyst Charlene Li bought a home, sold a home, remodeled the home she bought, and even rented a house as temporary quarters during the renovation period! In doing so, she used practically every real estate technology tool available to consumers—from the mainstay, MLS, to one of the newer kids on the block, Zillow.com. She chronicled her use and impressions of each technology on her blog (http://blogs.forrester.com/charleneli/2006/03/my_house_hunt_a.html).

Here is the list of the sites she used in her research:

- Craigslist.com
- HomePages.com
- MLSListings.com/Realtor.com
- Movoto.com (formerly iGenHome.com)
- Trulia.com
- Zillow.com

Forrester Research analyst Charlene Li says that Realtors by and large have embraced using technologies such as e-mail and digital photography to update their business practices. But the central premise of Realtors, as well as the MLS, is that they control the data and hence the process and the power. As new online tools tap into public databases— and more important, into the information that consumers themselves enter—more power will pass into the hands of the real estate consumer communities.

Do these new technology tools make the Realtor obsolete? Not at all, according to Li, but they do change the landscape. By empowering the consumer, these tools may change the Realtor's role from that of primary contact sales professional to more of a service provider.

While technology will have a significant impact, real estate is a complicated process, and making what easily could be the largest single purchase of one's life will not be something home buyers are likely do without professional help, especially if the other party is using the services of an agent. Most people will want to have someone with particular expertise at their side serving as an advocate and negotiator.

POSITION YOURSELF AS AN EXPERT

Thanks to advances in technology, the entire real estate industry is undergoing a fundamental, seismic shift, with more and more information available on the Internet. That shift will certainly have an impact on the role Realtors play as a result. The challenge will be to use all the tools at your disposal to capitalize on your expertise so that your clients will clearly see how important you are to the process! How do you communicate to prospective clients the benefits of your years of experience and intricate knowledge of the local market? One tool that certainly will help is blogging.

Blogs Help to Demonstrate Your Expertise

Blogs give brokers and agents a platform for articulating their viewpoints, knowledge, expertise, and experience with clients and prospects. This expertise can be with local neighborhoods, industry trends, home values, or other information of interest. Because they are updated routinely, blogs give Realtors an opportunity to be very current regarding their activities and to tell their own stories over and over again.

One marketing company, Backbone Media, suggests that the reason a Realtor should invest in using blogs as a marketing tool is not only because of the leads it will enable them to generate but because of the expertise it enables them to demonstrate. In a recent report, Backbone suggests that companies should invest in blog marketing because blogging will help them

- Demonstrate leadership in the industry
- Provide a connection to their audience and peers
- Start a wider conversation with their marketplace
- Use the Web to demonstrate their value message

In her book, *The Weblog Handbook,* veteran blogger Rebecca Blood says that the very act of blogging will help you to become an expert. "Whether you write about your avocation, your day, your business, or your take on foreign affairs, when you publish a blog, you are sharing information. As you research and write, you will gain an expertise in your subject," says Blood. "As you publish, you will accumulate a body of work, no matter how short the individual entries, and in this you create an online representation of your thinking."

We have learned the truth of this statement from our own experience. If you write about a particular subject long enough, you will gain expertise with it. Blogging forces you to stretch the limits of your knowledge and moves you to expand your comfort zone enormously.

Lenderama's Todd Carpenter says: "The number-one benefit to blogging is that it makes you an expert. Before I started blogging, I was just another good salesperson. Now, my opinion is being sought out by major publications such as *Investor's Business Daily* and *Inside Mortgage Technology*. Thanks to blogging, I'm now considered a recognized expert in my field."

Carpenter advises not to look at a blog as a sales call but as a source of information. Customers will want to work with you because of the expertise you demonstrate on the blog.

Blogging Boosts Your Credibility

Orange County Realtor Vince Bindi, who blogs at the "Orange County CA Real Estate" blog (www.ocrealestateblog.com), says: "Credibility is a benefit, but the challenge is conveying that to the public. Blogs enable you to do that in an efficient manner." He adds: "The expertise of the Realtor will always be of value, in much the same way as a stock broker. Your knowledge of the local market (home values, for example) is significant and is a case in point. But, unlike buying a stock, it is a complex process. There is a lot of detail." Bindi says that blogging gives the Realtor needed viability and legitimacy. "The old way was ads in the paper. The new way is blogging."

EXPERT'S TIP ➤ Learn from the Experts

One of the best ways to gain greater expertise is to learn from others who have already achieved a measure of it. Here are some resources we recommend:

> *"Real Blogging"* (www.realblogging.com). This real estate industry blog consists of more than 30 experts who post regularly on matters pertaining to the industry, covering every topic from advertising to technology.
>
> *"Realty Blogging"* (www.realtyblogging.com). This site is a network of blogging evangelists writing on effective real estate blogging.
>
> *"Inman News"* (www.inman.com/blogger/bradinman.aspx). This site offers real estate news and advice for buyers, sellers, and investors. The contributors include CEO Brad Inman and members of the Inman News staff.

HOW TO POSITION YOURSELF AS AN EXPERT

Here are some tips that will help you in using blogs to demonstrate your expertise:

1. *Write about what you know.* Use a blog as a platform to put your current knowledge into the public square. You do not have to be an expert at everything to start blogging; just start

with what you know. As someone wisely said, "You must begin where you are because you cannot begin where you are not."

2. *Write about the local community.* One of the areas where you certainly need to demonstrate expertise is with your local community. As Dave Taylor suggested earlier in this chapter, become a "community representative." Talk about the housing market to be sure but also about the community at large—local schools, sports teams, area business and industry, demographic data and growth trends, and even issues related to local government. Anything you can think of that might be of interest to home buyers, sellers, and local residents is fair game for your blog.

3. *Write about real estate trends.* What better way to demonstrate to prospects and clients your expertise in real estate than to share your thoughts, opinions, and ideas about current trends nationwide?

4. *Write about real estate technology.* We recently attended a real estate trade show where dozens of technology vendors were selling their wares. The amount of technology available to Realtors is overwhelming and growing all the time. The same is true of technology available to home buyers and sellers. It pays to become knowledgeable about the ins and outs of various technologies available. Use that knowledge to educate and inform consumers, and they will send their business your way because of it.

5. *Research, research, research.* If you blog routinely, it won't be long before you find yourself doing lots and lots of research, scouring real estate news sites, and subscribing to Google and Yahoo! news alerts, gleaning up-to-the-minute information. A large part of your research will be reading other real estate blogs, making use of the knowledge and expertise gained from fellow bloggers. Taking these simple steps will guarantee that your knowledge bank is never empty.

CONCLUSION

If you demonstrate that you are an expert, home buyers will seek you out when they need advice regarding a home purchase or sale. Realtors can be seen as experts who are selling value and professionalism. Using blogs to demonstrate your expertise provides you with a wonderful tool to attract more business, and proactively enhance your reputation.

Home buyers and sellers can now find "facts" more easily on the Internet, but what they can't do is make effective decisions without having "feet on the ground" in the person of an expert in the particular neighborhood or community in which they are interested. Consumers need a local expert in order to make fully informed decisions. Your blog is the best way yet to demonstrate your particular local expertise and make you the real estate agent or real estate company of choice for your community.

7

Relationship Marketing

Seventy percent of buyers who use the Internet in their home search start looking online six months to a year before making a purchase, according to the 2003 National Association of Realtors Survey of Home Buyers and Sellers. Capture the attention of these pre-prospects [with] one of the newest and most effective [tools]-the Web log, or blog.

Broker Agent News, November 2005

Farming is a term that Realtors understand very well. It's the practice of nurturing a neighborhood, getting to know the people in it, and establishing relationships with the goal that some will become clients when it comes time for a real estate transaction.

Traditionally, farming has been accomplished through a variety of methods: direct mail, knocking on doors, giving away promotional items, phone calls, and on and on. Let us add one more tool to your list of farming tools—a blog. Yes, that's right—blogs can be used to farm communities!

Paul grew up, not on a farm per se, but near several. In fact, all his uncles were farmers, and he had the "privilege" of working with some of them during his childhood and teen years (apparently, his parents were unfamiliar with child labor laws). Invariably, there were certain steps that had to be taken to grow a healthy, profitable crop. The first was to cultivate the land. This meant preparing the soil to receive the seed. It had to be plowed, fertilized, and sectioned into rows. Next came seed planting and then fertilizing. Each of these steps required careful nurturing and attention in order to ensure the production of the last step, a healthy, profitable harvest.

Real estate farming has parallels to its agricultural counterpart. You first have to "cultivate" a neighborhood, breaking the ice and getting to know its residents. Subsequently, you have to build relationships with the residents, which requires a great deal of time and careful attention. This is where blogging can play an important role.

BLOGS AS FARMING TOOLS

Using blogs as farming tools provides several unique opportunities, and also raises issues to be aware of concerning how to use blogs for the best results.

Informational versus Promotional

Realtors are becoming more and more Internet savvy. Blogs certainly are not the only online tool a Realtor can use to farm a community or neighborhood. E-mail may be another highly valuable one if you can get the addresses of residents and then get through their spam filters.

EXPERT'S TIP ➤ Case Study—Kevin O'Keefe

Blogs are an excellent replacement for e-mail and e-newsletters. Kevin O'Keefe of "LexBlog," a site that teaches law firms how to use blogs to market their firms (www.lexblog.com), recently reported that one of his client firms won the Legal IT Forum's "IT Innovator of the Year" award by demonstrating a "striking piece of lateral thinking by shifting away from standard e-newsletters to the world of blogging. From an original readership of 10,000, the winner's 'blogged' content now receives 600,000 hits and consistently appears on the first five hits for relevant search in Google and Yahoo!." So much for e-mail!

Blogs are a unique kind of marketing tool. They are "soft sell" machines. The language is informational, not promotional. It's like saying, "I just want to give you a heads-up."

Why does this distinction between an informational as opposed to a marketing or promotional focus exist, and why is it important? Blogs are considered by some to be the last form of honest communication. Blogging's history has its roots in honest, authentic, personal transmission of information, not "sales talk" or "marketingese." To come across sounding like a pitchman in the blogosphere will only win you enemies, not friends. While we realize that the market you're trying to reach is not bloggers, keep in mind that more and more people are becoming blog savvy. Let's face it; no one wants a sales pitch.

Jim Kimmons, a Taos, New Mexico, Realtor and blogger warns Realtors not to "heavy hand" their marketing via a blog but to keep it focused more on information. He says that if posts contain too much of a marketing emphasis, people will stop reading them.

Build Long-Term Relationships

Relationship marketing emphasizes the development of long-term rather than individual transactions. It focuses on the lifetime value of the customer. Blogs are an ideal tool to help foster such long-term relationships. They allow the customer to get to know you on a personal level, which can result in a sense of trust that you are who and what you claim to be. Blogs reduce the fear of the unknown. As you create that relationship through repeated interactions on your blog, readers, over time, are likely to gravitate toward you and your company.

Building a relationship like this takes time. By using your blog as a communication tool, while customers or prospects are getting to know you, you're connecting with them in a way that newsletters, with their unchanging static content, cannot. In fact, while this conversational approach is taking place, you are not "selling" them. You are not intruding and pressuring with a sales pitch. Instead, you're talking from the heart. You're speaking with passion and fervor about yourself, your business, your neighborhood, and what you have to offer. If you're good, you are also mixing in a little entertainment value and humor, making the blog not only informative but also fun. A blog is relationship marketing at its best. The blogger provides helpful information that benefits the readers. In return, readers express their appreciation with their home buying and selling decisions.

Blogs have increased importance as a retention tool. Blogs can be used to stay in touch with former customers, in lieu of postcards, newsletters, and magnets. Previous customers can keep up with what's going on in their neighborhood or the local real estate market via the blog, as you keep them updated with frequent postings. Using a blog for this approach is known as *pull marketing* as compared with the *push marketing* of direct mail. People get the information they want when they want it since they are coming to visit your site and you are repaid with repeat customer business as a result.

This is what relationship marketing is all about—building good long-term customer relations through interpersonal communication, but on a schedule that the customer wants. Blogs help you to achieve this goal in a way that no other offline or online communication vehicle can.

BENEFITS OF BLOGS VERSUS WEB SITES

Understanding the difference between a Web site and a blog is important. "Why," you may ask, "can't my current Web site do the same thing?" The truth is that without a blog component, many company Web sites are impersonal and uninviting to prospective customers and clients. Most often there is simply no effective connection made between the company and the potential customer.

In addition, most Web sites are static (unchanging) or updated infrequently. They give readers little reason to visit again and again. Ask yourself, "Why would a consumer who is not in the buying or selling cycle visit my regular static business site?" In fact, most will not!

On the other hand, a blog will provide a bridge between the consumer and your company by providing relevant, frequently updated information about a variety of locally interesting items. A site delivering fresh new content on a regular basis results in "stickiness"—the action of visitors coming back to the site again and again.

Just like any knowledgeable salesperson, as a Realtor, you know that it's easier and cheaper to *keep* a customer than it is to find a new one. Studies in several industries have shown that the cost of retaining an existing customer is only about 10 percent of the cost of acquiring a new one. Therefore, it actually makes economic sense to pay more attention to existing customers. However, it requires time and energy to stay "top of the mind" with your clientele. It is precisely the nature of ongoing interaction fostered by blogging that results in Realtors focusing on their blog as an ideal method to retain past clients, as well as to invite new clients!

Regular Communications

We've already mentioned that e-mail has its limitations, but even with those clients who willingly receive your e-mails, how often can you e-mail them? Once per month is a good number, but that's only 12 times a year. Can you keep their attention with this number of contacts?

Blogging enables you to fill in the gaps in terms of the number of contacts you make. If you post frequently, say, three to five times per week, you keep a constant stream of information available to clients and prospects. Some of them will even be technically astute enough to subscribe to your Really Simple Syndication (RSS) feed, so that your posts are streamed automatically to them almost in real time. (See Appendix E for further information.)

It's said that people need to hear an offer at least nine times before they buy. This is where a blog really can come in handy. Because it gives you the ability to tell your story over and over, a reader can be reached nine times with ease and many more times than that.

Blogs also include the comment feature that allows interaction between you and readers. Better than this, any time a comment is posted to the blog, most blog platforms will also send it to you via e-mail. Then, simply by hitting the "Reply" button, you will be conversing directly with the commenter. In other words, what began as a relationship online on your blog has now provided additional contact opportunities via e-mail or phone. In this event, the blog will have served as a match-maker—introducing you to a prospective client and then providing the means to develop that relationship.

Personalized Communications

A blog is personalized, one-to-one marketing that is impractical in any other format. Broadcast e-mail marketing isn't able to achieve this level of personally relevant messaging to your subscriber list. Adding a personal salutation, which is about all you can do to personalize a broadcast e-mail, isn't going to have the same impact as responding to a specific question or issue raised by someone who posts an inquiry on your blog. Using e-mails or newsletters that treat all your prospects the same will *not* resonate with the same effect. Having said all this, a coordinated campaign through the use of print newsletters, e-mail newsletters, and a blog is a good example of effective, coordinated multichannel marketing if you have the resources. If you cannot use all of the channels effectively, the blog is clearly the best choice.

For example, if you are farming a given neighborhood, one marketing piece might be a print brochure with your blog Uniform Resource Locator (URL; Web site address) on it. You use it to invite home owners to visit your blog for local news, events, and information, as well as updates on real estate trends, housing prices, etc. Occasionally, you also interject personal information and entertaining items. By integrating your offline print communications with your blog, your marketing message will be able to reach prior customers and new prospects in more ways than any single approach could accomplish.

Potential Content for Your Blog

Be sure to post several times each week. What do you write about? Well, write about anything and everything of interest in the neighborhood. Here is a just a short list to spark ideas:

Local News, Information, and Events

- School activities
- Fund-raising efforts
- New home construction
- Street repair
- Photos of landscapes

EXPERT'S TIP ➤ Use Listings with Blogs

While posting listings in your blog is not recommended by some real estate bloggers, there are ways to accomplish this without coming across as "over the top" selling.

- Annette Ashley Smith, a Florida Realtor, references listings when writing about her community. Rather than the listing appearing as the main topic of the post, she weaves it into the context of her commentary. Including listings in this way makes them seem less marketing-oriented and more like a natural part of the discussion.
- Another approach is to create a single blog per listing. This is what Realtor Jim Kimmons does, and it has several distinct advantages. The blog provides more room for detailed information than an MLS listing allows. It provides greater exposure for the listing, with lots of photos and text. Technically savvy readers can subscribe to the blog's RSS feed, and it has residual effect for search engine exposure. There is also a cross-linking benefit from multiple blogs linking to each other and to the main Web site, which allows for the buildup of high-quality links. In addition, the property owner can submit blog posts or leave comments, creating a greater sense of participation by the property owner in the sales process. In essence, the blog becomes an interactive, online brochure for marketing the listing.
- One final approach is not to include listings of particular properties but to post upcoming open houses. This has the benefit of educating the consumer without appearing promotional. Todd Carpenter, expert blogger at Lenderama.com, says that an open house is "an event, rather than a listing. By mentioning open houses in your blog, you're providing more information than sales."

Real Estate News

- Current trends in the marketplace
- Home-buying/selling tips
- Current home prices

Fun Stuff

- Occasionally inject some puzzles
- Games
- Funny stories or photos

Make it family-friendly and entertaining. (If you need some inspiration on how to do this, check out www.moosetopia.com, a blog by ice cream manufacturer Denali. It's loads of fun.)

Listings

This is your call. There is a split in the real estate blogosphere as to whether it's a good idea to include your listings. Some believe that it makes the blog just another sales site that will turn visitors off. Others simply note that not including them would be a lost opportunity to generate interest in your current home offerings. At the very least, you *must* include a link to your listing database.

COMMUNITY BLOGGING AS A FARMING TOOL

What else can your blog farm consist of? Earlier, we described Community Publisher product offered by Blogging Systems, LLC. The Community Publisher is designed to include community *member organizations* such as charities, civic groups, schools, chambers of commerce, senior citizens groups—the list goes on and on. Each of these individual groups is the basis for a different kind of "farm." In fact, this product has been called the most exciting approach to farming ever developed for the real estate industry! Why? It's because every one of the members of these various groups and associations represents an opportunity to build your brand through a twenty-first century "farming" approach. Here's how it works.

The real estate company, team, or agent, as the community sponsor, will have many farms, each identified as a member of the overall community. The blog home page will provide access to each individual member's blog. Individual agents or staff members within the company's centralized marketing department may have the opportunity to be the personal contact for a particular group or association, based on personal interests.

For example, one farm might be a "Little League farm." You meet with the head of your local Little League and provide him or her with a free blog on the community blog as a participating member. The blog has a calendar of events including the games, schedules, award ceremonies, fund raisers, etc. The Little League farm individual blog might also include league standings, won-lost records, and news of outstanding performances by the kids. Of course, you go to the games, introduce yourself to the managers, and ask if they would like to write about their players on the blog. You ask age-appropriate kids and their parents if they want to post some content about the games. Getting the idea? You "own" the Little League farm. Every contact is an opportunity to build a relationship. In the world of marketing, this is brand building of the highest order.

The list of participating groups is almost infinite. In the category of athletics, other possible farms might be the Pop Warner Football League, local high school teams, etc.

The local chamber of commerce participation opens up a huge number of relationship opportunities, since each company member in the chamber can have its own blog. Of course, as the blog sponsor, you go to the next chamber of commerce meeting to discuss what the community blog is all about, how easy it is to blog, and the successes that others have had participating on your blog! Then contact the local Rotary Club, Lions, etc. Keep going and going and going.

Other examples of potential farming groups include senior citizens groups, government agencies and departments, clubs and organizations, charities, civic groups, etc.

Interested in becoming the local destination site for real estate-related services? Start a different type of community. Instead of members being part of an association or an organization, create an "affinity" based community. Invite local real estate-related companies to participate—law firms, mortgage companies, painters, plumbers, title companies, etc. The list can be endless. Invite your community's residents to post comments about good experiences they have had with your community bloggers. How many times have you heard people complain about how hard it is to find good, reliable contractors? Your blog could provide meaningful recommendations and referrals to local vendors from trusted neighbors and community members. On your community blog, bloggers could canvas their customers and post testimonials, and the vendor portion of the blog might even include a rating system.

Can you think of any current medium that can get your name and brand in front of so many people in a way that presents you as *the* local involved Realtor specialist in the community? This is relationship marketing beyond anything currently existing in the marketplace.

To determine the outcome, you need to have time for the word to get out. Your neighborhood residents will begin to read your blog. As they get to know you and learn of your expertise in real estate and knowledge of the neighborhood, it is likely they will tend to call on you when they have a need to buy or sell a home. It all depends on how well and how often you communicate. Your blog must provide value to the reader in order to encourage return visits. What if other Realtors are farming the same neighborhood using traditional farming techniques? Your blog gives you a leg up because you are able to create more connections more often than your competition.

BE INNOVATIVE IN YOUR MARKETING TECHNIQUES

Have you ever walked into a crowded restaurant and tried to get a seat at someone else's table? Probably not, but that's what Realtors do with their marketing efforts every day. Farming neighborhoods and communities using the same methods as everyone else gives you zero visibility in a very crowded marketplace. A better idea is to get a table of your own. By this we mean, rather than using the same tactics and techniques as everyone else, be innovative and try something no one else in the marketplace has tried. Come up with ideas other people have yet to think of.

Business Benefits of Blog Farming

- *Grow your list of prospects.* Your blog can become a lead-generation tool more valuable than any other. Because of the personal interactions blogs facilitate, prospects and clients will respond to you with comments and e-mails.
- *Create long-term customers.* Your readers will come to know you and your organization. Over time, you will have the opportunity to develop lifelong relationships with your blog participants, especially with a community blog open to all.
- *Gain increased customer loyalty.* Blogs establish a relationship through regular personal contact with your site. The result will be that your customers will stay loyal.
- *Establish customer referrals.* Not only will customers stay loyal, but they will also become referral sources for you. These "brand evangelists" will promote you and your company to family and friends.
- *Get your message out.* You and your company can get your message out in a timely fashion to the widest audience possible and in a manner in which *you* want it presented.
- *Control the flow of information.* Rather than relying on press releases or major news stories to present your organization's announcements, your messages can be delivered in smaller releases over time. This allows you to better control the flow of information while obtaining feedback and consensus along the way.
- *Maximize marketing of events.* Posting your events and activities on the community calendar maximizes the exposure and marketing for those events by reaching the largest community audience possible.
- *Demonstrate your unique character.* Blogging will help you to better demonstrate its unique character and personality. It

allows you to reach out and touch the community in a manner that is more personal and real.

Community Benefits of Blog Farming

Equally important are the benefits that will accrue to your community if you invite active participation—all of which builds closer ties with clients and prospects. Here is how Realtor David Crockett lists the community benefits:

- Your blog will crisscross your community in a thousand different ways and become the "watering hole" for local news and information.
- Your blog will provide your community with "juice" and energy and help bring people together in a way that is fun and interesting.
- Your blog will give your community life and personality. (People and businesses looking to relocate to your area can visit the blog and see a lively, vibrant community with personality that offers opportunities and activities, picture scrapbooks of events, and so much more.)
- Your blog is a living, real-time mosaic of your community. (Visitors won't have to Google search in order to discover information about your community. It's all right there in one large town hall open house.)

CONCLUSION

This may sound like a lot of work, but *it is not!* If you establish a relationship with a blogging platform company that specializes in real estate blogs there is a very simple, easy-to-follow process that gets you started with a week-by-week plan—particularly if you have a community blog. Once your blog is up and running, it will establish a life of its own, with other community members and readers providing most of the content. For those who recognize the value of building deep and lasting relationships in your local market, these special and unique approaches to "farming" can produce remarkable results.

The blogging phenomenon has yet to achieve mainstream adoption among Realtors, but this is rapidly changing. Being a "first mover," especially with community, organization, and affinity group blogs, has an enormous advantage because once a particular community is established in a local market, it is unlikely that the same community will have another. For personal blogs, this is not a problem because each personal blog will have its own "voice," and with practice and attention, your blog can be the best!

8

Exploiting the Niches

*The mass of niches can be found in Web logs. Any company look-
ing to reach their customers today will need to join in on the conversations happening on Web logs.*

—BILL FLITTER,
CMO, Pheedo.com

The day of mass marketing is over. The market is splintered into a million
and one different pieces. The old paradigm was to design a marketing
message in such a way as to attract as many people as possible, hoping
that at least some of those people would filter through and become customers. Marketers would send their messages to as many people as they
could afford to through as many different means as possible (e.g., television, radio, print, etc.). The problem today is that people are being so
inundated with disruptive, uninvited messages that they don't even
remember them, much less respond. Not only that, but consumers are reg-
ulating their intake of marketing messages, time shifting them using technology tools such as TiVo and iPods. Thanks to these tools, people may
not even hear or see the message at all!

There is a better way: Let your initial message do its own filtering.
Design it in such a manner that it appeals only to a narrowly defined market. In this way, the people it is intended for will lock in on it. This is called
niche marketing. As a Realtor, you doubtless understand that marketing in

Figure 8-1. Wailing Wall in Jerusalem.
(Photo Credit: iStockPhoto.com.)

today's landscape is all about penetrating and exploiting niches. Blogs can help you to do this very well.

Dr. Ralph Wilson, who many call the "godfather" of Internet marketing, uses an illustration of the Wailing Wall in Jerusalem to describe this phenomenon (see Figure 8-1).

If you stand at the base of the wall and look up, it seems like a massive monolithic structure. However, if you look more closely, you see cracks between the stones. If you look even more closely, you see slivers of paper, dozens of them, stuck in the crevices. These are prayers of the faithful who visit the wall.

Perhaps large companies have the scale and budget to cover the entire "wall of the Internet," but small businesses do not. As a Realtor with a smaller marketing budget, you may feel at a disadvantage. You are not. There's no need to scale the entire wall. You only need to fill one crack. It's all about finding a niche and exploiting it, and blogs can help you do this.

DEFINE *YOUR* NICHES

Dr. Wilson suggests that you take a look at yourself or your company and ask some questions:

> *What are you good at? What do you enjoy? Is there a particular niche of the real estate market in which you might be considered an authority? What are your strengths? How can you leverage these strengths? What do you have to offer that is unique? Instead of fantasizing about the "perfect," take what you know and let it empower your vision to clearly see the niches out there.*

A blog enables you to write on a regular basis about your core competencies. These competencies can be defined as your niches. If you can exploit a yet-to-be-filled or only partially filled niche, your message has the potential to spread quickly by virtue of the technology inherent within

---

EXPERT'S TIP ➤ Blogging Thrives When Serving a Specific Niche

According to Dustin Luther of the "Rain City Guide," both real estate and blogging thrive when they effectively serve a local and/or niche market.

> [T]he idea behind this should really be second nature to successful real estate agents who know they couldn't possibly serve all the niches within a major city. Rather, my experience has been that successful agents will say that they began by providing exceptional service to a small subset of people. Maybe their niche involves houseboats or condos or a specific neighborhood. . . . The specific niche doesn't matter. The important aspect is that a real estate agent realized that they were never going to be able to serve everyone well, so instead they focused on a small subset of people and learned that market inside-and-out [www.raincityguide.com/2006/04/10/relevance-is-at-the-long-end-of-the-tail/].

most blog platforms. With proper promotion and some "sweat equity," your blog can become a powerful sales and marketing tool.

According to advertising technology expert Paul Beelen, advertisers must understand the "last mile" of marketing. This means that advertising is not solely about standing out but rather about delivering messages that reach "microtargets," or audiences that ensure relevancy. Niche blogging enables advertising messages to be targeted specifically at those people who are likely to find the message relevant.

The National Association of Realtors "Web Wizard Report" from as far back as 2002 noted the following:

> *Since they often attract readers interested in narrowly focused subjects, blogs can be ideal tools for Realtors who specialize in niche markets. Blogs can be created that focus on the housing needs of retirees, first-time home buyers, or pet owners or on trends in the retail industry, new urbanism, waterfront communities, home offices, synthetic leasing, the continuing controversy over power lines, etc. Such Web logs would help show potential clients the Realtor's expertise in working with specific types of properties and transactions* [www.realtor.org/webintell.nsf/pages/33].

"Blogs could end up providing the perfect response to mass media's core concern: the splintering of its audience." This is one of the closing salvos to *the* article on business blogging to date (*BusinessWeek,* May 2005). The article goes on to say: "Advertisers desperate to reach us need to tap niches. . . . By piggybacking on blogs, they can start working that vast blogocafé, table by table. Smart ones will get feedback, links to individuals—and their friends. That's every marketer's dream."

BusinessWeek has thrown down the gauntlet. Mass media is archaic. Reaching a mass audience is no longer a viable marketing strategy. Now the mantra is, "It's the niches."

GEOGRAPHIC NICHES

There are over 82 million Google results for the term *real estate blog.* Realtor and expert blogger Jim Duncan (www.realcentralva.com) says: "Competing with the large national blogs . . . takes time, money, and most importantly, *teams*. Real estate is a local business, influenced greatly by macro factors, but ultimately no two markets are alike. The best real estate blogs find their respective local niches and run with them." Figure 8-2 is a sample post from Duncan that focuses on his local geographic niche, with information that his community will find highly relevant. Notice the "facts" with a little bit of "personality" thrown in.

In a manner of speaking, every Realtor serves a niche market. Because your business is local, you can have a geographically based niche. How, then, do you use a blog to exploit that market? One way is to become more knowledgeable about your area than anyone else. Focus your blog's content on your target market, and provide as much information as possible. Include information about local schools, restaurants, transportation, and shopping centers. Discuss current real estate market trends, and within the context of talking about your community, show listings and homes you have sold. Your blog will help you to demonstrate your knowledge of the area and the industry and, in addition, serve as a tool to motivate home buyers and sellers to choose you over other Realtors serving the same area.

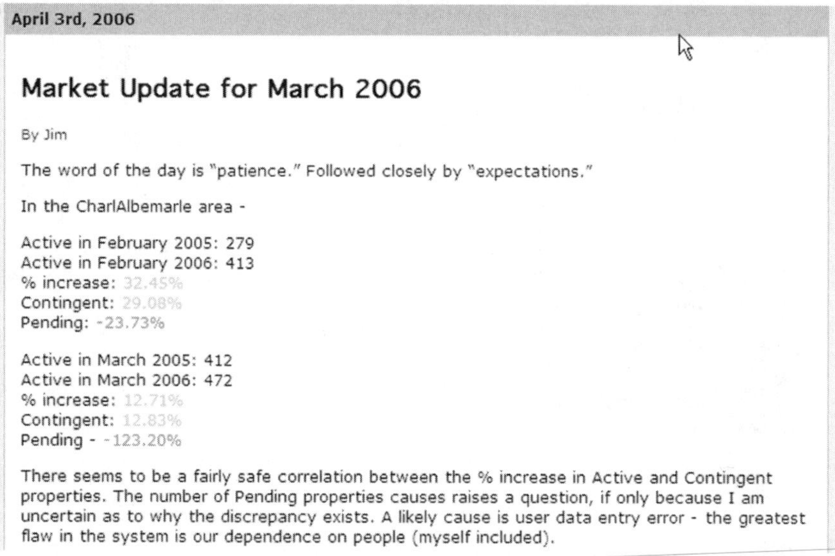

April 3rd, 2006

Market Update for March 2006

By Jim

The word of the day is "patience." Followed closely by "expectations."

In the CharlAlbemarle area -

Active in February 2005: 279
Active in February 2006: 413
% increase: 32.45%
Contingent: 29.08%
Pending: -23.73%

Active in March 2005: 412
Active in March 2006: 472
% increase: 12.71%
Contingent: 12.83%
Pending - -123.20%

There seems to be a fairly safe correlation between the % increase in Active and Contingent properties. The number of Pending properties causes raises a question, if only because I am uncertain as to why the discrepancy exists. A likely cause is user data entry error - the greatest flaw in the system is our dependence on people (myself included).

Figure 8-2. Post from Jim Duncan's blog showing market analysis.

Having a well-defined geographic niche market enables you to deliver more compelling sales messages. Most home buyers begin their search in a large metropolitan area with broad criteria in mind. As their research continues, they begin to get an idea of where they would like to live, what properties they can afford, and which real estate company they can go to for assistance. The key is for you to stand out from others in that area and be the Realtor of choice.

If you live in a large metropolis such as New York or Chicago, a blog about the entire city usually would not qualify as a niche. Narrow it down to a few neighborhoods or subdivisions. You'd be amazed at the amount of information you can share on a weekly basis just at that level. Niche targeting also helps where Internet searches are concerned. For example, suppose that a prospective buyer is interested in purchasing a home in the Berkeley Hills area of California. A real estate agent who is the "Berkeley Hills expert" obviously will be considered a much better choice than one

Figure 8-3. Blog post from Orange County Realtor Vince Bindi.

who is "serving the San Francisco Bay Area." And, while there may be hundreds of thousands of search engine page returns for San Francisco real estate, the number would be much less for a more well-defined, smaller area, giving you a greater opportunity to stand out.

Targeting specific geographic areas, whether they are neighborhoods, towns, or counties, probably is one of the most popular ways Realtors are using blogs these days. Web searches can find geographically oriented real estate blogs blanketing the country from Portland, Oregon, to Tampa Bay, Florida.

Realtor Vince Bindi is just one example of a blogger who targets a particular geographic area. Touted as the Orange County's "premier real estate blog" (www.ocrealestateblog.com), his blog (Figure 8-3) provides information about housing trends, home prices, market statistics, MLS home searches, and buying and selling tips for Orange County, California.

EXPERT'S TIP ➤ USE YOUR BLOG AS YOUR GEOGRAPHIC NICHE

Realtor Vince Bindi of Orange County, California, states: "Our focus is only south Orange County, which is a conglomeration of small cities. We will pick a city—there are about 12 in the area—and provide stats on it, how many homes are on the market, how active the market is, and new developments that may be going up, if any. We don't do a lot of national issues but choose to stay local in focus." Regarding choosing a niche, Bindi suggests that Realtors "look to see what you enjoy writing about in your local community, including things beyond real estate." He also advises determining the purpose or game plan of your blog before you start it.

PROPERTY NICHES

Many home shoppers looking for real estate information online will seek out markets associated with specific types of properties. Here are several property-type blog approaches.

Luxury Market

Do you serve the luxury market? This is a perfect blog niche. Not only can you write about homes in your area, but you also can write about other topics that might appeal to the people living in the area. Real estate marketing expert Tim O'Keefe says, "Niche marketing is about finding an underserved market and then entering the conversation going on in their head." Take a cue from a blog such as "Luxury Portfolio Blog," an all things "luxury" blog (www.blog.luxuryportfolio.com), for content that might be appropriate to the upscale audience.

Figure 8-4 is a sample post from the "HauteBlog" (www.hauteblog .com), which focuses on luxury real estate and design.

Figure 8-5 is another sample luxury-related post from Annette Ashley Smith's "Sarasota Real Estate News," which focuses on luxury homes and resort-style living in Sarasota, Florida.

New Home Developments

Does your neighborhood have a lot of new home developments? We all know of the explosion in new development building in recent years. These

Figure 8-4. Post from Haute Blog.

SATURDAY, APRIL 08, 2006

Buy a House for your Boat!

Your boat needs this private dock, along with the wonderful views down the canal from this two bedroom, two bath Sarasota, Florida home. It's a boater's dream with water views from all rooms and magnificent sunsets.

This home offers a den, large living room, dining room, kitchen with newer appliances, free-standing ice maker, Florida room and more. What a convenient location to beaches, shopping, golf, fine dining, Sarasota downtown condos and cultural activities. Seller says boating water is excellent with no bridges to Bay. For the best of Sarasota Real Estate, check out this $1,295,000 home at our main website.

posted by Sarasota Realtor @ 5:48 PM   0 comments

Figure 8-5. Post from Sarasota Real Estate News blog.

new home owners will be your neighborhood's sellers at some point. Target and farm these communities, and you will own this "farm" until you retire! You can create your own localized new construction blog and partner with builders, attorneys, or title companies. If your company works closely with participating builders, you might consider starting a blog together with those builders focusing on news and information regarding upcoming and existing new home developments. Including this type of blog in a larger community blog would maintain home buyer visits to your blog site even after the new construction closes.

Established Neighborhoods

Is your target-market neighborhood an older community? Offer a home-improvement blog. Partner with local contractors to offer regular tips on making a home more appealing. Encourage site visitors to comment on these tips and make their own recommendations. Over time, a community blog revolving around this simple niche will thrive. Figure 8-6, the "Bob Vila Construction Project Blog," is a sample that you may consider as a model (www.bobvila.com/BBS/Construction_Project_Blog/flat-page1.html).

Second Homes and Investment Properties

Are there a lot of investment properties or second homes in your market? If so, provide investment analysis tips, information on being a landlord, or tax tips on renting second homes. Partner with a local accountant and financial planner to be sure that your content is accurate, and use these connections to increase your offline community building further with those partners. Second-home and investment-home buyers are likely to be avid Internet users, and Google searches for second-home and investment-home blogs did not return many relevant search engine results,

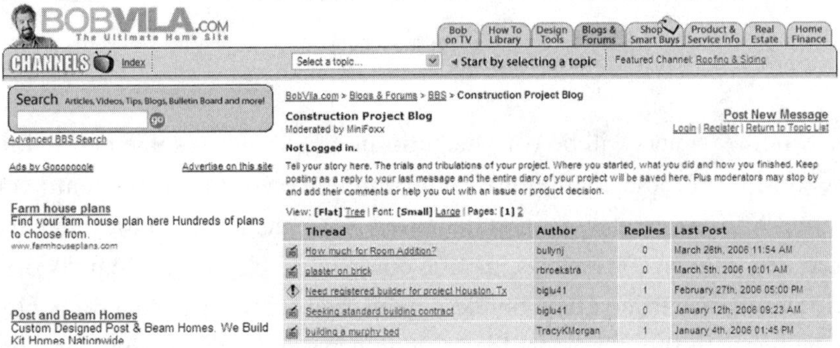

Figure 8-6. BobVila.com Web site.

April 1, 2006

Net Present Value of a Property
By KevinKingston

A great article that basically points out the Ben Grahm and Warren Buffett way at looking at investments and applying it to housing. I'll go one further; applying it to any property or any business venture would send your success rating through the roof! This is the way to evaluate any investment like Warrenn Buffett.

Read the NY Times article here.

Othe articles and sites on the subject:

Figure 8-7. Post from Real Estate Investor's blog.

Figure 8-8. Post from Vacation Home Insider blog.

so this is a niche available for anyone willing to take the time to create a focused blog with lots of related links. Figure 8-7 is a sample post from Kevin Kingston's "Real Estate Investors Blog" (www.bloglines.com/blog/ KevinKingston).

Figure 8-8 is a sample post from Grace Lichtenstein's "Vacation Home Insider" blog (www.vacationhomeinsider.blogspot.com). Grace is a former *New York Times* reporter and author who has written extensively on travel and real estate.

MEMBERSHIP NICHES

If you belong to membership organizations, bring them online with you. Contact your alumni organization. Universities are usually very support-ive of alumni. If you are a member of a real estate-related trade group or affiliated association, participate in its blog if it has one, and if it doesn't, suggest creating one.

Join or create a panel of experts on a topic relevant to real estate or another topic of interest to your community. For example, the "Realty-Blogging" community is a "network of blogging evangelists writing on effective real estate blogging." The "Real Blogging" community (www. realblogging.com), created by RealtyU and Blogging Systems, LLC, con-sists of a forum for industry leaders to discuss all aspects of importance to the real estate industry.

ETHNIC NICHES

The growing diversity of the U.S. population presents special opportuni-ties for niche bloggers. The U.S. Census Bureau estimates that in 2005, 31 percent of the U.S. population consisted of African-American, Hispanic, Asian/Pacific Islander, and Native American residents.

One of the fastest-growing population segments is Hispanic. Accord-ing to real estate marketing expert Tim O'Keefe, "The Hispanic community is a widely untapped, underserved niche for the real estate professional." He provides these statistics (http://houseblogger.typepad.com):

- The population of Hispanics will grow to 103 million by 2050.
- Currently, one of eight Americans is Hispanic: 66 percent from Mexico, 14.5 percent from Central or South America, 9 percent from Puerto Rico, and 4 percent from Cuba.
- The Hispanic market will be worth $200 billion in new business in 2007.
- Hispanic-owned businesses will grow 55 percent by 2010.
- Hispanic purchasing power will grow by $12 trillion by 2010 (bigger than Mexico's gross domestic product).

More specific to the real estate industry, a 2003 comment from the Congressional Hispanic Caucus Institute, quoting the U.S. Census Bureau, says the following:

The home ownership rate for Hispanics in the United States (46.1 percent) continues to lag significantly behind the nation's overall rate (68.1 percent), as well as that of non-Hispanic whites (74.6 percent). Over the past 10 years, however, Hispanic rates have improved, and in some cases Hispanic homeownership has grown at a rate three times higher than that of other non-Hispanic groups.

A report from the University of Southern California (USC) entitled, "The Homeownership Potential of Mexican-Heritage Families," cites these figures: "84 percent of Latino renters 'strongly' desire to buy a home and 55 percent plan on buying in the next five years. As a result, the Tomas Rivera Policy Institute (at USC) estimates at least 1.5 million Latino households will buy homes by 2010."

According to Juan Guillermo, an expert marketer serving the Latino community,

Latinos are buying more and more homes and those companies cashing in on this trend are the ones taking the risks and making the necessary efforts to provide those products and services that the Hispanic community was lacking in some degree: closing documents in Spanish, title insurance, mortgage loan services, sheer information on the entire home buying process [http://juantornoe. blogs.com/hispanictrending].

Another reason for you to pay attention to this market is that Hispanics are becoming more Internet-savvy. For example, eMarketer projects that the number of Hispanic Internet users in the United States will rise from 13.3 million in 2004 to 16 million in 2007.

Hispanic branding is crucial for real estate brokers who wish to attract Hispanic clientele. Creating a Latino-friendly brand is a first step toward creating a lasting relationship with Hispanic buyers and sellers. A blog addressing the housing concerns of the Latino community will greatly assist real estate brokers in establishing these relationships. This is an absolutely untapped market and is open to first movers in communities across the United States.

One blog that targets the Hispanic market with real estate news and information, "Ahorre" (www.ahorre.com), is shown in Figure 8-9. Although the site does not deal with real estate exclusively, it covers such topics as California real estate agents, housing prices, and real estate investment opportunities.

According to *The Mercury News* (www.mercurynews.com/mld/ mercurynews/living/special_packages/homebuying/11574091.htm), California is seeing a dramatic increase in ethnic home buyers, and local real

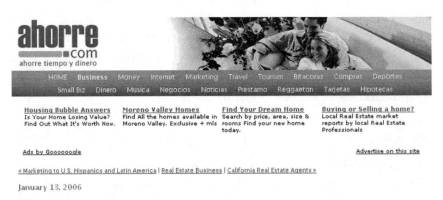

Figure 8-9. Hispanic blog Ahorre.com.

estate agents and associations are responding to this increase in a variety of ways:

- The Santa Clara County Association of Realtors created several ethnic Realtors' organizations in the past two years, including ones for agents who are Filipino American, Vietnamese American, Indian American, and Hispanic.
- First American Title rolled out a new marketing program to reach minority real estate agents, is planning seminars that address the needs of Asian home buyers, and is launching a Web site in June aimed at Asian consumers.
- Most developers, including Shea, KB, and SummerHill homes in Palo Alto, employ Chinese *feng shui* principles in their home designs.

The Mercury News quoted Derrick Hall, senior vice president of communications for KB Homes, as saying that in 2004, immigrant home buyers purchased nearly half of the 32,000 homes sold nationwide by KB.

These ethnic niches currently are underserved by the real estate blog market. A search for blogs focusing on ethnic niches found almost no results. This means that the opportunity to move first and capture this target market with a blog that resonates with special ethnic groups is within anyone's grasp.

GENDER-BASED NICHES

Research suggests that women are responsible for most home-buying decisions. Marty Barletta, author of the book *Marketing to Women,* notes, "Women are responsible for 83 percent of all consumer purchases:

- Home furnishings (94 percent)
- Vacations (92 percent)
- Houses (91 percent)
- Consumer electronics (51 percent)
- Cars (60 percent influence and 60 percent of purchases)"

This niche includes both married and single women. "Single women are getting tired of waiting for prince charming," says Tacoma, Washington *News-Tribune* reporter Barbara Clements, who maintains a real estate blog called "Open House" (http://b2e.thenewstribune.com/index.php?blog=13). Clements asserts that single women are buying houses in record numbers.

According to the 2004 National Association of Realtors "Profile of Home Buyers and Sellers," the single-female segment of the home-buyer population accounted for 18 percent of all home buyers in 2004. Single women purchased approximately one in five homes in 2003. In the same year, one in ten was purchased by single men. During the time period from 1994 to 2002, the number of unmarried females owning homes climbed from 13.9 million to 17.5 million.

AGE-BASED NICHES

Seniors over the age of 65 represent one of the fastest-growing segments to embrace the Internet. Internet use among this group has jumped 47 percent since 2000. Since e-mail is the top Internet-related activity for seniors, there's every reason to conclude that blogs also can be a very effective niche opportunity to reach the senior market.

Another fertile category is the baby boomer group, which is now reaching retirement age in record numbers and makes up the largest buying group in America. Baby boomers certainly are Internet-savvy. They use technology in their work and for pleasure as well. They shop online, book travel online, communicate online, read online, and therefore are likely to be most receptive to a blog that targets them as a special niche.

Not only that, but boomers are buying up houses at a record rate, and not just one home. A report from the National Association of Realtors states that nearly 40 percent of all homes bought in 2005 were second homes, up from 36 percent in 2004. Who is purchasing these homes? Affluent baby boomers. Typical vacation-home buyers were 52 years old and earned $82,800 a year, whereas the median age for buyers of investment property was 49, with an income of $81,400, according to the survey.

GAY AND LESBIAN NICHES

One of the most educated and affluent population segments in America is the gay and lesbian community. According to Tim O'Keefe, the annual value of this market is $515 billion.

Here are some more statistics cited by O'Keefe:

- 21 percent of gay and lesbian households have incomes greater than $100,000 per year.
- 28 percent have incomes greater than $50,000 per year.
- 62 percent own a personal computer.

One Denver-based company, Gay Real Estate, Inc. (www.GayReal Estate.com), recently launched GayGhettos.com, a nationwide database of gay and gay-friendly neighborhoods in the United States. The site takes submissions from users to add information about these neighborhoods. Figure 8-10 is an example of the blog that addresses issues related to gay home ownership and gay-friendly communities. This is yet another example of an underserved niche.

Figure 8-10. GayRealEstate.com Web site.

CONCLUSION

A blog is a superb niche-targeting tool. The key to its success is finding a niche in which you are very comfortable and about which you can speak authoritatively and passionately. Try to widen the possibilities, and be creative—commercial real estate, buyer's agent only, land only, international—these are all other opportunities. If the niche fits, target it with a blog, and watch your business grow!

9

Media and Public Relations

The new world of the blogosphere is a great opportunity for PR and brands. Markets are interconnected as never before.
Guide to the Blogosphere, Edelman and Technorati

Paul recalls the first time it happened. He was busy working away on his computer when a call came from the *Philadelphia Enquirer.* At first, he thought it was the *Enquirer,* the gossip paper found on grocery store checkout aisles. He quickly googled the phrase *Philadelphia Enquirer* and realized that it was a reputable, leading newspaper. The reporter on the other end of the line wanted to interview him for an article she was doing on blogging.

This was the first of many such interviews conducted by leading newspapers, magazines, and even the *Wall Street Journal.* How did they find him? Why were they calling him? *One reason only*—his blog.

Paul is a business blog consultant. The only way he has ever marketed his business is through his blog. He uses the exact same concepts and ideas that we are describing throughout this book. He writes frequently, passionately, and knowledgably about this new media revolution called *blogging.* The result? High search engine returns and calls from members of the media who are hungry to write stories about blogging. The media find him through search engines queries!

MEDIA USE OF BLOGS FOR SOURCE MATERIAL

Journalists are now often using blogs for source material. One study done by public relation's firm Euro RSCG Magnet shows that more than half (51 percent) of journalists use Web logs regularly for source information, with 28 percent relying on them for day-to-day reporting. Of the journalists who use blogs in their work, 53 percent use blogs to find story ideas, 43 percent for research and referencing facts, and 36 percent for finding sources.

"The findings of this . . . study simply validate what we have known for some time: that blogs are playing a more significant role in the way information is transmitted to readers and journalists alike, and may profoundly alter the media and communications landscapes," said Aaron Kwittken, CEO of Euro RSCG Magnet. "The fact that the media are using blogs for reporting and research also demonstrates that blogs have an enormous potential to not only influence the general public, but to influence the influencers—journalists and the media—as well" ("Eleventh Annual Euro RSCG Magnet and Columbia University Survey of the Media," www.magnet.com/index.php?s=_thought).

Realtors are experiencing this same kind of activity. Realtor David Crockett has seen evidence of this from his "Lake County Blog" site. The newspaper article mentioned previously is a perfect example of a community blog entering the media's field of vision and being written about. Shortly after the "Lake County Blog" went live, Crockett's local newspaper ran an article on the community blog entitled, "Lake County Enters the 'Blogosphere.' "

> *"About 90 million blogs are currently in existence," said David Crockett of the Mentor-based Crockett Team of Howard Hanna Smythe Cramer, which launched the site. Some estimates put the rate of expansion of what's known as the "blogosphere" at one new blog per second.*
>
> *LakeCountyBlog.com is of particular significance, Crockett said, because it's the first of its kind in the county, and a collection of blogs on one Web site has advantages over each organization creating a blog of its own.*
>
> *For more information, visit* www.lakecountyblog.com.

It's hard to imagine that Crockett's site could have received better press if he had written the article himself. Further, Crockett reports to us that since the article was written, he has met with the publisher of his local newspaper, who recognizes that the community blog represents an opportunity. They have agreed to work together, and share marketing efforts. Talk about the media coming to you instead of your soliciting the media for attention.

EXPERT'S TIP ➤ Gain Media Attention

Jonathan Miller, president and CEO of Miller Samuel, Inc., a New York real estate appraisal firm, maintains two popular real estate blogs, "Matrix" (http://matrix.millersamuel.com) and "Soapbox" (http://soapbox.millersamuel.com), which have garnered quite a bit of media attention.

> Most of the people that cover the real estate market here read my blog a number of times during the week because every time they call me, they are telling me about stuff they read on it, which is great. They know what I am thinking, and they know whether it is worth coming to me for a story because they understand my depth of understanding about some issues. It also is a resource, and it triggers story ideas for them. I have had a number of times that that has come up.
>
> For example, I had a situation that happened in the third quarter of last year. I write a series of market studies on the Manhattan real estate market, and they are used by the Fed, the IRS and the lenders and Wall Street firms. It was on the front page of the *New York Times*. They basically used my study to call the crash, which was picked up around the globe.

Figure 9-1 is a good example of how the media can help to build your position within the industry.

Here's what the media says about Jonathan Miller

- Why is Jonathan Miller's Matrix required reading? ...He grabs you right from the start - *The Walk-Through (NYT)*
- our sherpa in the land of broker euphemism for the current state of the housing market -*The Real Estate (New York Observer)*
- a combination of Godzilla, King Kong, and Hurricane Katrina all wrapped up in one as he wreaked havoc on the housing market -*The New York Sun*
- [Jonathan Miller's] third quarter 2005 report, for a blizzard-like example, perhaps single-handedly - and unintentionally - ended the housing boom, not only in the city, but nationwide - *The Real Deal*
- Jonathan Miller, a chartist and a real-estate artist -*Curbed*
- Somebody-explain-this-crazy-market-to-me guy Jonathan Miller -*Curbed*
- a Curbed reader goes all *Jonathan Miller* on us - *Curbed*
- ...assessment of the real estate market and not only features moi but the great Jonathan Miller. - *Property Grunt*
- Jonathan Miller is definitely one of the hottest real estate bloggers around. - *Rain City Guide*
- market guru Jonathan Miller - *Brownstoner*

Figure 9-1.   Media responses to Jonathan Miller's Matrix blog.

Alex Stenback, author of the "Behind the Mortgage" blog, has received his share of media attention as well, from both local sources and national publications such as *Investors Business Daily* and *Kiplingers.* Stenback says that the "buzz" from his blog resulted in an opportunity to host his own radio show, a two-hour Sunday morning program on a local talk-radio channel dealing with money matters. Stenback says, "Attention from the media was an unintended but welcome consequence of blogging."

SOME NEW BLOGGERS ARE JOURNALISTS

Real estate blogging has gotten the attention of the media to such a degree that many journalists are getting in on the action. As noted previously, Barbara Clements covers the real estate beat in her "Open House" blog for the Tacoma, Washington, *News-Tribune.* In fact, when considering what kind of blog to start, the newspaper chose one covering real estate rather than one more consumer-oriented site. Clements covers the real estate beat from a local perspective but writes about national trends as well. Her real interest is in exploring the impact of home ownership on home buyers and their families. It has to do with "people and their dreams," shares Clements. "People are making the biggest purchase of their lives, and there is a lot of emotion attached to that. People put passion into their homes."

Even the ubiquitous *New York Times* has seen the value of real estate blogging. When considering what blog content to include in its original set of blogs, the *Times* started one entitled, "The Walk-Through" (http://walkthrough.nytimes.com), authored by a team of real estate bloggers (see Figure 9-2). As to why real estate, "The Walk-Through" blogger Damon Darlin said, "There is an incredible amount of interest in real estate among *Times* readers, and we saw the blog as one more way to present information." Darlin continued, "Because the newspaper is circulated nationwide, the blog covers news from a national perspective. . . . Topics tend to be rather eclectic, covering issues such as economic trends, housing trends in various localities around the country, problems in markets, as well as lifestyle issues."

Business Week—the publication that screamed in May 2005 that "Blogs are not a business elective. They're a prerequisite" has itself started

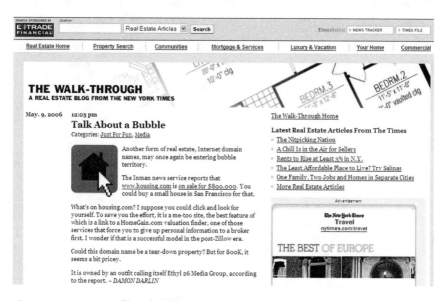

Figure 9-2. New York Times blog "The Walk Through."

a real estate blog, "Hot Property—The real story on real estate" (www. businessweek.com/the_thread/hotproperty; see Figure 9-3). Authors Peter Coy, Dean Foust, Toddi Gutner, and Chris Palmeri say, "We scan the blogosphere so you don't have to." Rarely a week goes by that they don't refer to and link to other real estate bloggers.

The power of blogs as a public relations and media communication tool is so strong that the *Wall Street Journal* is reporting that companies that see the value of blogs are

> . . . *looking for candidates who can write in a conversational style about timely topics that would apply to customers, clients and recruits. Blogging as a job has emerged as companies of all stripes increasingly see the Web as an important communication venue. Blogs allow firms to assume a natural tone rather than the public-relations speak typical of some static Web pages, and readers are often invited to post comments. While some companies are hiring full-time bloggers, others are adding blogging duties to existing marketing or Web-editing positions* [Wall Street Journal Online, *May 31, 2005*].

Figure 9-3.   Business Week's real estate blog "Hot Property."

Public Relations Companies Use Blogs and the Pull Model

Media and public relations (PR) companies are now beginning to move away from the outdated paradigm of the *push* model, where the press release is the main source of client information dissemination, to the *pull* model, where PR firms set up RSS feeds and blogs to allow client content to be distributed openly to a wider audience that *wants* to receive it. Figure 9-4 is a sample of Blogging Systems, LLC's, PR company Misukanis & Odden's list of RSS feeds it issues on behalf of its clients. This enables Web site visitors to receive news and information when they want it by subscribing to only the content they are interested in.

The lesson to be learned from all of this is that you need to be publishing your content in a way that will appear on the media radar, and a blog is the perfect tool to do exactly that.

Figure 9-4. Misukanis & Odden public relations firm blog.

YOU AND YOUR READERS AS MEDIA

A revolution is taking place in media and public relations. Consumers are writing their own blogs and writing on other blog sites and delivering the message better and more effectively than any other advertising medium. At the same time, mainstream media are confronting their own problems, and the level of trust in the media is being tested. In addition, the consumer is wary of top-down, command-and-control corporate communications. Four of five people say that they would refuse to buy goods or services from a company they do not trust.

The most recent Edelman "Trust Barometer," which tracks the opinions of influential people about credible sources of information, lists a "person like you" third, only behind physicians and academics, as a credible source of information. Just a few years ago the trust level in peers was only about 20 percent. Today, it's 68 percent. Richard Edelman calls what we are now experiencing the "Me2 Revolution" era of communications. He explains this pattern as

> . . . the network of cross influence. The network is a dynamic, real and virtual world of information exchange in which all participants demand a voice. Those who have been at the bottom of the pyramid of influence-consumers and employees-are the new influencers, and they use an array of new tools that enable them to share information and opinions online [Edelman/Technorati, "Public Relationships: Communications in the Age of Personal Media," winter 2006].

Newsweek recently ran a cover story entitled, "Putting the 'We' in Web." Some noteworthy reflections by the magazine include

- "What makes the Web alive is, quite simply, us."
- "It's the main news source for the non-arthritic population, and a megaphone for those who make who their own media."
- "It's not an audience, it's a community."

"Media is fragmenting; consumers are taking back control," says Pete Blackshaw, chief marketing officer for Nielsen BuzzMetrics

(KansasCity.com, *The Kansas City Star,* March 14, 2006). Marketing expert Paul Beelen says

> *It is very clear that traditional media are losing their grip on their audience. As a result, consumers will be extremely difficult to reach, as they will be scattered all over this landscape of micro-content. Instead of reading the mainstream local newspaper, they will read micro-content written by someone with the same interests they themselves have.*
>
> *. . . today's hyper fragmented media landscape allows for micro-targeting to ensure [the] relevancy of commercial message. Instead of targeting huge target groups through expensive television or print ads, companies can now target their messages more specifically.*

David Kline, coauthor of the book *Blog!,* has this to say:

> *The fact is that consumers are no longer willing to put up with shoddy products, indifferent service, and lack of accountability and transparency. What's more, they are demanding a decision-making voice in shaping the products, services and media they consume. TiVo is one example of this new take-charge attitude on the part of consumers. Indeed, the consumer now demands more of business—and thanks to blogs and other new consumer–empowering technology and media—he can now get it. Companies who meet these new expectations are rewarded. Those that don't will see their businesses punished as never before.*

Essentially, we live in an era where trust in peer-to-peer communications is at an all-time high. Blogs have entered the mainstream as a crucial supplement to press releases and traditional forms of advertising. Thanks to the Internet, consumers have been empowered like never before. The mere fact that a new blog is created every single second speaks volumes. The hard truth is that *people talk.* And they are talking about you and your services in chatrooms, on message boards, through instant messages and e-mail, and yes, on blogs. Because we live in an age called *participatory journalism,* everyone can be a reporter, a reviewer, and a critic. Everyone has a voice, and thanks to the Internet, those voices are now being heard!

EXPERT'S TIP ➤ Communicate without "Pitching"

Transparency is the key. Blogs are not another way for you to make a "sales pitch." Speak in a conversational manner, and address your readers as you would in an e-mail to a friend. Be authentic. Edelman describes two schools of PR thought. The first relies on psychological insights into audiences based on control. The other theory, known as the *Arthur Page theory,* is focused on telling the truth and listening. Blogs, based on the foundations of honesty, interesting content, and fresh new material, present a compelling case for the Arthur Page approach to effective public relations.

Engage yourself with customers and prospects. Leverage the "comments" facility of blogs to encourage and maintain public exchanges of information and ideas. Move away from selling toward conducting a continuous dialogue with the goal of learning what your readers and prospects want and need from their local real estate expert and then responding to those wants and needs to the best of your ability.

Tell stories. People love stories. Use a blog to tell the story of you and the story of your company. Great bloggers convey their own individual experiences and views. You are the expert in your domain. Use that fact to engage with, learn from, and collaborate with the widest possible audience in your target market.

Connect with other bloggers. Word of mouth from other bloggers is by far the most effective means by which to attract attention to your blog. Bloggers trust other bloggers, as seen in Figure 9-5. By engaging other bloggers in a meaningful, worthwhile dialogue, you create enthusiasm and goodwill regarding your blog. The value of endorsements (and links) from other bloggers is immeasurable.

Here are some of the differences between the old world of PR and the new from Edelman:

Established Approach	Emerging Model
• Tightly Controlled Message	• Move from Control to Conversation
• Elites Get Top Billing	• Allow Consumer to Co-create
• Speak at—Not with—the Audience	• Transparency
• The Company Knows Best	• Wisdom of Crowds

How, then, can you as a Realtor get your message heard in a way that consumers will respond to favorably? It certainly demands that you adapt to these new ways of thinking about marketing. Blogs have the ability to create a dialogue, start conversations, and talk and listen to clients, prospects, consumers, and the media. A blog provides a direct link from your real estate company to the outside world. The blog can be the "real voice" of your company, speaking and responding in a conversational environment with your specific market universe.

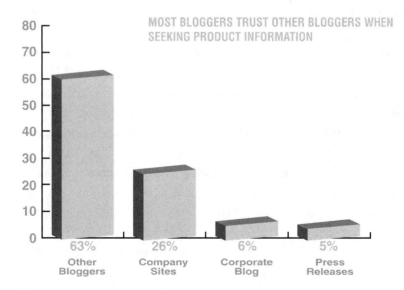

Figure 9-5. Chart from Edelman/Technorati "Public Relationships" report. (Edelman/Technorati, "Public Relationships.")

Real estate and all that comprises its universe—including the housing bubble, house values, property taxes, etc.—is a conversation topic of great interest. After all, for most people, there is no single purchase a family makes that is deemed more important than a home. The best and most interactive way to get involved in this ongoing conversation is by becoming a blogger yourself.

MANAGE YOUR OWN ONLINE REPUTATION

As your blog grows in readership and exposure, you need to start tracking what others, including the media, are saying about your blog. Monitoring the blogosphere is important because these conversations about you and your site will not always include a link to your site or a comment on your site.

Those people "talking" that we mentioned earlier—the Internet has given them the ability to share their opinions about your company or experiences they've had with your company publicly in a way never available previously. If what they are saying is good, that's helpful to your company. The Internet and especially blogs have put word of mouth on steroids!

How you or your company is defined these days is often in the hands of third parties. It's beyond your control. Research shows that 39 percent of the top 100 search engine returns are driven by what's known as *consumer-generated media* (CGM)—content created by and shared among consumers, not companies! Further, blog search engine Technorati reports that over 87,000 blogs include the term *kudos,* 65,000 have *boycott,* and over 100,000 contain *scam* in the blog name. Companies that put time and effort into managing and building their reputations make a huge mistake if they turn a deaf ear to CGM.

As consumers shift their focus toward online research, the importance of knowing what other people are saying about your company increases exponentially and is as important to small companies as it is to the corporate giants. With consumer-driven review sites such as "Judy's Book" (www.judysbook.com) or "Yahoo! Local" populated with reviews from customers, it is more important than ever for small businesses to keep a close eye on their online reputation.

In addition to review sites, RSS feeds and blog *aggregators* (blog sites that gather content from various other blogs and post that content in their own blog format) are making it easier than ever for individuals to share their thoughts and experiences with the world. With tens of thousands of blogs going online daily, businesses no longer can afford to ignore the comments of their customers. A disgruntled customer ten years ago might have shared his or her anger with family and friends; now, such a customer has the ability to publish the experience for the entire world to see.

Monitor Other Blogs

In addition to participating in conversations within your own blog, it is vitally important that you are also tuned into the blogosphere in terms of monitoring what's being said about your company and your brand. Search engines such as Feedster, Technorati, IceRocket, and PubSub, which monitor and index millions of blogs, can track these postings, and you can search these engines for information about you and your company.

You also can create custom RSS feeds based on keyword searches and use an RSS reader to keep track of these keywords. What you track with RSS is everything related to your company, such as your company name, your name, key industry phrases, etc. You can do this tracking with a bevy of free tools from Google Alerts (www.google.com/alerts), Yahoo! Alerts (http://alerts.yahoo.com), Blogpulse (www.blogpulse.com), Feedster (www.feedster.com), and Technorati (www.technorait.com). Figure 9-6 is a Feedster RSS feed result for "RealtyBlogging." Figure 9-7 is the Google Alert for "Realty Blog."

Surveying the blogosphere for negative messages can help to serve as an early warning system for you and your company. Chances are that what bloggers are saying today, journalists and the media will be saying tomorrow. If you can "head them off at the pass," it will be to your advan-

Getting Links To Your Blog
Feedster on: realtyblogging
Conversation: Getting Links To Your Blog
Posted: Tue 5/9/2006 1:24 AM
Posted To: Feedster on: realtyblogging

http://feeds.feedburner.com/Sellsius?m=89

Thanks to Richard Nacht and our friends over at Realtyblogging for this great link to an informative Google Blogoscoped questionnaire. (Contributed by Chris Bubny) It's a must read for every blogger who wants to increase links to their blog posts.

Related...

Figure 9-6. Feedster RSS feed for RealtyBlogging.com.

tage. Not only do you need to know what is being said about you and your company, but it's also important to know what's being said about your competitors.

Online business and competitive intelligence can keep you ahead of the curve. The challenge is that on the Internet, the curve is moving all the time. What is being said about you and your company in blogs, forums, and news groups can have a lightning-fast effect. You always need to have your finger on that pulse.

Actively Cooperate with Other Bloggers

Building a positive relationship with bloggers also can help companies not only when the going gets tough but also when it is time to spread buzz

Google Alert - realty blog
Google Alerts [googlealerts-noreply@google.com]
To: rnacht@gmail.com

Google Alert for: **realty blog**

Sugar Pine **Realty : Blog**
From Open Houses to Sold Homes. We've been the leading real estate office in the Sonora, California area. We are Real People Providing Premier Service.

Real Estate Marketing **Blog**
Marketing advice and commentary for the online **Realtors** success. Real Estate **Blog** Directory Use for listing your real estate **blog**; Real Estate MLS Listings ...

Beautiful Santa Barbara **Blog**
Texas Real Estate **blog** · HomeBlog™ Your Home **Blog** for your family, Real Estate **Blog** and Home News · **Realty** Baron · Southwest Florida Real Estate ...

Figure 9-7. Google Alert for "Realty Blog."

about new products or services. Reaching out to bloggers by including them on your press release list, posting comments on their sites, and engaging them through e-mail contacts will help to forge positive relationships. If you've found a well-read blog that pays a compliment to your company, take the time to send a thank-you. This might be an e-mail or a snippet of news or information that the blog can feature on its site. Consider adding the blog to your blogroll. (You will be surprised at how a small act on your part will pay big dividends because many are likely to reciprocate by driving activity to your blog in return.)

Consumers get to know bloggers in an intimate way, and trust is fostered as a result. This means that if they recommend something or are enthusiastic about it, that endorsement will resonate with the highest level of intensity.

Deal with Negative Blog Comments—ASAP

If you find a negative comment on a blog or forum, treat it the same way that you would treat any other public relations issue. Look into the complaint, and if it is fixable, fix it. If you can't fix it, create a blog post that links to the complaint, explain your side of the story, and describe the steps you are taking to address the problem. Don't sweep it under the rug—"Nip it in the bud" while there is still time to do so.

It's difficult, if not impossible, to completely control your message in the world of the Internet. By becoming proactive—keeping abreast of what is being said about you and your company and taking the steps suggested here—you will give yourself the best opportunity to ensure that the reputation you and your company have is the reputation you want.

CASE STUDY: Kryptonite

Delay in responding to negative posts can have disastrous results, as evidenced by the experience of Kryptonite, a bike lock company. The company was famous for its tough locks that were thought to be impenetrable. In September 2003, someone demonstrated online how you could open the lock with a Bic pen. The news traveled quickly through the blogosphere five days before the *New York Times* and other mainstream media picked it up.

Kryptonite largely ignored the blogosphere during that five-day window, issuing only a statement that the locks were completely theft-deterrent. By the time the news hit the mainstream media, the company had a huge PR problem on its hands. The problem reportedly cost the company $10 million, nearly half its annual $25 million revenue. Had the company paid more attention to the blogosphere and responded earlier, disaster might have been averted.

CONCLUSION

Media attention may be an unintended consequence of blogging but one that should be welcomed. While you may not be featured on the cover of the *New York Times,* blogging can vault you into the limelight at an even more important level from a career perspective—the local community you serve. Share your knowledge, expertise, and insights on a blog, and the local media most assuredly will beat a path to your door with even more opportunities to raise awareness of your brand in your marketplace.

10

Lead Generation

Please contact me with more information.
Reader comment left on a
blog post at "Urban Trekker"

Our discussion thus far has revolved around how blogs can be used effectively as tools for branding, niche marketing, search engine optimization, and more. Although these are very important, of even greater importance is to turn all the traffic, search engine presence, and increased Google PageRank into new business! In the world of sales and marketing, this is called *lead generation.* In Internet parlance, it's called *conversions.* It does little good to have traffic if that traffic does not translate into something more tangible, such as an e-mail contact, phone call, or other type of actionable item with the potential for additional business transactions.

To say that lead generation is important to Realtors is like saying that sunlight is important to plant growth. A steady flow of qualified leads is the lifeblood of any successful sales professional. To meet this demand in the Internet age, real estate technology sites such as Home-Gain.com, HouseValues.com, and RealEstate.com, as well as many others, have appeared.

ESTABLISH CUSTOMER RELATIONSHIPS

Traditional lead-generation systems are designed to highlight comparisons and give users the opportunity to compare features and benefits of different real estate companies and different real estate agents. This approach is a *competitive perspective.*

An effective blog, however, *establishes meaningful relationships* with its readers. The sole purpose is to create a substantive bond based on qualities of trust, goodwill, respect, mutual appreciation, and open communication. For most people, the purchase or sale of a home is the largest financial transaction of a lifetime. Isn't it easy to understand that for a transaction of this importance most would prefer to do business with people they know and trust and with whom they are comfortable?

Types of Approaches

There are several different approaches real estate industry bloggers take in establishing meaningful relationships. "Behind the Mortgage" blogger Alex Stenback focuses on providing content rather than delivering an overt sales pitch. In Stenback's case, his goal is to "develop a readership and establish relationships in order to stay top-of-mind with people" so that they are likely to contact him when they need a mortgage. Clearly, even with an information-oriented blog, client acquisition is *always* on his radar screen. As shown in Figure 10-1, the site also contains a prominently placed banner ad ("blogvertisement" he calls it) encouraging visitors to contact him when they need a mortgage.

Stenback projects that the blog will be responsible for a large increase in his business. "Last year, I did about three to four million in direct business. I believe in 2006-2007 that number will be much higher as a result of my blog, both in actual loans and in other business opportunities writing a blog can create."

Dustin Luther of "Rain City Guide" feels that blogs can provide Realtors with leads that are more qualified than those provided by standard lead-generation systems: "Thanks to the blog, readers send very personal leads. By the time they e-mail Anna [his Realtor wife], they feel they have a relationship with her already. Rather than just a sentence

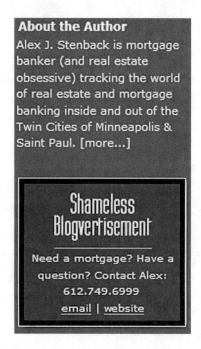

About the Author
Alex J. Stenback is mortgage banker (and real estate obsessive) tracking the world of real estate and mortgage banking inside and out of the Twin Cities of Minneapolis & Saint Paul. [more...]

Shameless Blogvertisement

Need a mortgage? Have a question? Contact Alex: 612.749.6999
email | website

Figure 10-1.   Banner ad from Alex Stenback's Behind the Mortgage blog.

or two about what they're looking for in a Realtor, Anna will get 10 to 15 paragraphs about what their life is like [family, job, etc.]." To Luther, it is the personal nature of blogs that creates this level of trust and familiarity. Figures 10-2 through 10-4 are just a few samples of comments left on the "Rain City Guide" blog from prospects who wanted more information (*Authors' note:* We have purposely chosen short samples for the sake of brevity.)

SpiderWorkz.com president and real estate lead-generation specialist Tim O'Keefe describes how he *positions* a blog. He suggests there are two goals for a blog: "One goal is to create a sense of authority and credibility in your market, and the second is to capture leads." These two goals are not in opposition to each other because a blog can provide a platform for both. He says that it is not enough for a blog simply to generate traffic. At the end of the day, a blog is a Web site, and any Web site can generate visitors. It's what becomes of the visitors when they arrive at the site that differentiates a blog from a static Web site. O'Keefe believes that a

I also found your site by searching google for "living in seattle".

My husband and I may be relocated to the Seattle area early next year and were trying to find information on some of the suburban areas. We would need to be about 40 min to an hour at most away from downtown Seattle. We are looking for a relatively small city (under 30k people) with low crime and good schools.

We are moving from California (although not the bay area) so hopefuly Seattle will welcome us as well.

Figure 10-2.   Comment written on Rain City Guide blog.

There seems to be a common theme here. I also searched Google for "living in Seattle".

I'm considering moving from Southern California, but I would be coming with my dog & having to rent an apartment without having a full-time job yet. Do you think I could afford an apartment on temp salary until I found a full-time position, or is that financially unrealistic?

Thanks!

Figure 10-3.   Comment written on Rain City Guide blog.

8. **Kate – January 1, 2006**

any suggestions on cities to live in within reasonable commute time to downtown seattle?

Figure 10-4.   Comment written on Rain City Guide blog.

Web site, whether static or blog, must create leads in order for it to be considered an effective marketing tool. O'Keefe doesn't think that Web surfers are looking for blogs—he believes that they are looking for meaningful content and that those sites that provide useful content will generate interest, comments, and contact information if given the opportunity. By positioning your blog as a site with valuable content, you automatically get more opportunities to capture leads owing to your increased visibility in the search engines.

To best demonstrate how blogs can be used as a tool for lead generation, O'Keefe cites the first time he visited Las Vegas. He remarked to a cab driver that getting around the city required a great deal of walking. He remembers clearly the cabbie's response: "Remember, all roads lead

EXPERT'S TIP ➤ Blog for Leads

Tim O'Keefe offers these helpful tips on successful blogging for lead generation:

Look at a blog as you would a real estate farm. When farming, everyone targets a specific neighborhood or niche market. Your blog should become an online farming tool. Focus your blogging on the neighborhood you are targeting by sharing pertinent information about it.

Write about things that matter to people. Take local issues and write about them. This might include special events going on in the community, homes for sale in the given neighborhood, and even such things as property tax rates or zoning restrictions. Demonstrate your knowledge of the area you are targeting.

Occasionally include posts about national issues such as interest rates, the housing bubble, or the time it takes to sell a home based on market conditions. This demonstrates your knowledge of the real estate market generally.

When you write, editorialize and have an opinion. Take a stand, create expert opinion, and make a case for the position you take. This further builds credibility and authority.

Write about properties and offer listings, whether they are all your listings only or all available local listings. Use the blog to offer teasers of listings, and then redirect the readers to your MLS site. "The main thing homebuyers are looking for are houses for sale," says O'Keefe, "and I highly recommend providing them [with] this information."

We add the following:

When you write, invite comments and feedback. Your site will be more inviting to visitors when it contains interesting "threads."

Remember that the most fruitful "farming neighborhoods" for developing important relationships may not be a physical group of homes at all, but organizations or associations as previously discussed. By broadening your perspective in this way, a whole new world of "farming" opportunities opens up.

through the casino." Using blogs for lead generation is no different, says O'Keefe. "All roads must lead to a registration page or some other type of lead-capture tool."

West Orange, New Jersey, broker Ken Baris of Jordan Baris, Inc., also attests to the need to have lead-generation mechanisms in place on your blog. He says that many Realtors are now blogging for the purpose of blogging but suggests a better use: "Don't turn the blog into your business; turn your blog into a business generator."

EXPERT'S TIP ➤ Capture Contact Information

Here are just a few ideas for capturing lead information. Visit our Web site at *www.realtybloggingbook.com* for ongoing tips and hints on blogs as effective lead generators.

- Include your toll-free number on every page of your blog.
- Provide a contact form so that your readers can contact you as the site sponsor, in addition to leaving comments on your blog.
- Have an e-mail newsletter subscriber option.
- Offer a free competitive market analysis.

USING YOUR COMPANY WEB SITE

You may be saying, "but I already have these lead-generation features on my main company Web site, so why should I repeat it on my blog?" The fact is that a blog *is* a Web site, albeit of a different variety. It is not an either/or proposition, but a both/and proposition. There is no question that home buyers and sellers are going to the Web to look for information about properties to buy or sell, and they aren't stopping after viewing any single site. Your regular business Web site is now competing with all types of new lead-generation technology tools. You need to place yourself in as many places on the Web as possible to capture prospect information. Unless you can be sure that Web visitors will get to your main Web site when searching for local information or properties, it makes sense to apply some of the same lead-generation efforts to your blog to give yourself the greatest opportunity to convert Web visitors into clients. In addition, as noted in a variety of ways throughout this book, your blog can create a greater degree of trust in you and your services by enabling you to manifest your expertise—this will result in a greater degree of willingness on the part of your blog visitors to provide you with contact information as compared with your regular business Web site.

CONCLUSION

Your blog cannot help but be a lead generator when you have used it to establish yourself as the local expert and/or the community-site sponsor. No other marketing tool allows you to build a rapport gradually with your site visitors like a blog. Its purpose is to build you and your company to a position of "top of mind awareness" when your visitors are ready to consider a real estate transaction. This is the essence of effective branding.

11

Intranet and Project Management

Blogs were once the domain of angst-ridden teens and doomed presidential candidates. But the likes of Verizon, IBM, Microsoft and Dr. Pepper are all climbing on the blogwagon. Turns out, Web logs are a nifty knowledge-management tool.

Fast Company

Real estate organizations that can benefit from the use of an internal (intranet) blog include Realtors in a single-office real estate company, multioffice brokerage companies, and regional and national membership trade associations.

All of these groups face a daunting task—that of communicating effectively and efficiently with their members. While some organizations use some type of intranet application, others are forced to rely on e-mail as the main vehicle for internal communications.

There are problems associated with both approaches. Often, traditional intranets are expensive to purchase and maintain and difficult to use. E-mail is fraught with problems, thanks to unsolicited commercial e-mail (spam) and filtering technologies used by Internet service providers (ISPs). Because there is no one benchmark to which all ISPs subscribe, a sender can never guarantee that a particular e-mail campaign will reach all of the intended recipients. Not only that, messages sent via e-mail are difficult to archive, and the conversation thread is difficult to follow.

Is there a better way for organizations to communicate? Indeed there is. Blogs have proven themselves to be effective alternatives to the more traditional approaches, offering many benefits to the organization. In fact, some of the best known Fortune 500 companies, including IBM, McDonald's, and DaimlerChrysler, are using blogs just for this purpose.

Here is a brief synopsis of some of the advantages to using blogs:

1. Blogs are easy to use. If someone can send an e-mail or create a Word document, he or she can use a blog.
2. Blogs offer infinite archiving of data by both date and category.
3. Conversation threads are easy to follow. One person posts a message, and other stakeholders can respond quickly and easily using the comment function built into the blog interface.
4. Blogs are useful for committees or project teams. These entities can set up and maintain their own blog, to which any or all of the stakeholders can contribute. Further, owing to the comment functionality just mentioned, blogs allow for interaction between members.
5. Information is displayed in reverse chronological order. The newest information always appears at the top.

According to the National Association of Realtors' 2002 "Web Wizard Report":

> *Realtor associations can benefit by creating Web logs for members. A Web log can be a cost-effective supplement or replacement to a monthly member newsletter, providing information on and links to new forms and regulations from the state licensing agency, educational opportunities, meeting announcements, policy changes, legislative updates and calls-to-action, and links to relevant articles and Web sites. Blogs may also be used to keep committee members informed and updated on projects and developments. In every case, the blog can be updated whenever new information becomes available; there's no need to rely on production schedules or how quickly the mail can be delivered.*

Both intranet blogs and outwardly facing marketing blogs use basically the same type of software. The main difference from what we've previously described is that because intranet blogs are designed for internal use, they are often password-protected.

BENEFITS TO INTRANET BLOGGING

Shel Holtz, principal of Holtz Technology & Communications, says that "whatever succeeds on the Internet will find its way to the intranet." Much of what we've written about the effective use of blogs as a marketing tool also applies to "internal" communications.

Ease of Use

Before the advent of blogging technology, many existing intranets were not used in the way they were intended because the existing software was often difficult to learn and required participants to fit their information into inflexible existing categories. Current blog technology is easy to use with a very simple learning curve. If you can create a Microsoft Word document or send an e-mail, you can create a blog post. Any and all authorized users can participate. Mike Wing, IBM's vice president of Internet strategy, believes that their simplicity and informality could give them an edge in office communication. "It may be an easy, comfortable medium for people to be given permission to publish what they feel like publishing" (*Fast Company,* April 2004).

Simplicity

One key to the usefulness of blogs for intranet purposes is that they don't require vast information technology (IT) resources to get them up and running. Most blog platforms can be installed easily and quickly on the organization's server *or* are what's known as *hosted solutions,* requiring no onsite installation. This bodes well for real estate brokerages or associations that may not have internal IT resources or a large budget to devote to this.

Further, blog platforms tend to be incredibly stable. They require very little ongoing maintenance or upkeep. This is not to suggest the absence of technical difficulties. It's just that the evolution of blog plat-form technology has led to the creation of very reliable software.

In addition, the administration of intranet blogs is relatively simple. Using a blog, such things as setting user privileges and administrative lev-els and creating categories and other setup features can be done in just a few minutes. This permits information to be created and posted quickly in an efficient manner. In many blog platforms, categories can be added in real time as the blog post is being written. And thanks to the program-ming language used in creating blogs, even changing design templates is accomplished with relative ease.

Cost-Effectiveness

Blogs are not expensive to deploy. Sophisticated content management sys-tems (CMSs) can cost many thousands of dollars, whereas a Movable Type license, for example, costs only a few hundred. Some blog platform solutions such as WordPress actually cost nothing except the time needed to install and configure the software.

Technology company Infoworld (www.infoworld.com) was pre-sented with a quarter-million-dollar quote by a vendor for an intranet portal application, even though the need for such an expensive piece of software had not been identified within the company. After further dis-cussion, the company opted for a blog solution instead.

Regarding the decision, Chief Technology Officer Chad Dickerson said, "Our internal use of Web logs has greatly accelerated, and we're beginning to see more tangible benefits as we've begun to reach a critical mass of internal contributors." The company now considers the use of blogs as "indispensable."

Archiving of Information

Think about the information currently stored within a typical organiza-tion. Isn't some of it trapped in e-mail boxes that no one will ever see again or stuck in long-forgotten databases? Blogs support infinite archiv-ing of information by both topic (category) and date. Most blog platforms allow content to be searched as well, making blogs the perfect tool for managing the intellectual property of an organization. Files associated with blog posts can be stored within the blog for later retrieval.

E-mail Saver

According to Nicholas Tang, director of operations at Community Connect, an online builder of U.S. ethnic community sites, the deluge of work-related e-mail messages can be overwhelming. "It got to the point where I was getting hundreds of e-mails a day, sometimes more than a thousand" (*New York Times,* July 7, 2003). Community Connect's solution was to implement a blog. Mr. Tang's engineers send content updates to their private blog viewable by the authors and their managers, including time and date stamps and often with links to relevant Web sites. "When I want to know something I check the . . . [blog]. It saves me the trouble of e-mailing people or yelling across the room to get a status update." A blog accomplishes these results without filling up e-mail inboxes all across the organization and/or work groups. Intranet blogs also eliminate the scourge of e-mail—spam. In a password-protected environment, only real and appropriate content can make it to the blog site.

Build Community

Blogs can be used to establish a sense of community within an organization. An intranet blog can give voice to many authorized individuals and allow each to publish content on his or her blog. In addition, such posts also can be added by each individual to the overall community blog and assigned to specific categories or topics. An intranet community blog can create a social environment within the walls of an organization or association that enables staff to connect in a manner unavailable in any other online medium. This community emphasis can have its own business purpose. It is particularly important in many real estate offices where all agents are not available to attend all meetings or where a company has many agents working virtually.

BlogCentral, an internal IBM blog program, enables employees to keep personal blogs. Brian Doyle, a spokesman for IBM says, "We're a company of experts. We're about encouraging these people to interact,

and that leads to breakthrough thinking and innovation" (KansasCity
.com, March 14, 2006).

Intranet blogs are unlike most corporate intranets in that they are a
bottom-up approach that fosters wide staff participation. "With blogs,
you gain more, you hear more, [and] you understand where things are
going more," according to Halley Suit, who wrote a fictional case study on
corporate blogging for the *Harvard Business Review* (*Fast Company,* April
2004). This permission-based content levels the playing field within the
organization and allows all staff members to feel like part of the team.
Think of your intranet blog as a town square where your staff meet,
"speak," and interact more effectively and more often than previously
practical.

MAKE USE OF YOUR INTRANET BLOG

Now that we have covered a number of benefits to using blogs for internal
communication, how can they be put to work in actual practice? Here is a
short list.

Alerts

How does a real estate brokerage or association notify members when
there is an important announcement or time-sensitive update? Traditionally, an e-mail broadcast would be sent. The problem with e-mail is that,
thanks to spam filters, there is no way to guarantee that the message will
be received by every recipient. While this means of communication certainly is still valid, blogs provide an adjunct method. The responsible
party simply writes a blog post. Every member who has subscribed to that
blog's Really Simple Syndication (RSS) feed will receive the message.

Project Management

Project teams working in a group blog environment can easily maintain an
ongoing record of decisions and actions. Project leaders also can use the
blog to keep other company personnel current with respect to the status of
any given project. According to IBM researcher Dan Gruen, "We've seen

people using blogs to diary their daily experiences using a new technology or building a new kind of system, monitored by others as a sort of real-time virtual apprenticeship, which lets them observe events as they unfold and see the issues that arise and how they are addressed" (InfoWorld.com, March 28, 2005). This approach is far superior to the traditional approach characterized by mountains of records in file cabinets.

Departmental Notification

Department heads can use blogs to notify company employees of current activities and achievements. A marketing department can submit a post announcing the availability of a new marketing brochure. Because files can be uploaded, the new brochure can be available on the blog for everyone in the organization to read.

Company and Industry News

The blog can become a repository for company or association news, press releases, industry-related news, and current trends. Thanks to its ease of use, both management and employees can contribute.

Brainstorming

One of the best uses for intranet blogs is as a collaborative tool for brainstorming new ideas. There are a number of ways this can work. The project leader (or committee chair, as the case might be) can write the initial post, and other members can respond via the comment component. A blog even could be set aside just for brainstorming purposes, with each member contributing as an author. As with all things blog, information can be categorized by topic, date, or author.

Personal Blogs

A personal blog can prove valuable to an organization in so many different ways. Consider a broker who reads a lot and attends several real estate conferences and conventions. She can update her blog with summaries of the articles she's read and notes she took at the conferences. All of the readers who find value in this information will read the blog and pass the information along.

CEO and Key Staff Blogs

A blog is a wonderful way for the CEO and other senior management personnel to get closer to employees. Imagine a new CEO hosting a blog called "My First Hundred Days" in which he or she writes about daily experiences and lets employees comment in order to help him or her get acclimated. Other key people within the organization can blog about their specific area of responsibility in an environment that encourages sharing and participation by all.

Share Best Practices and Training

Blogs can be used to share best practices, tips, and other announcements about new technologies or marketing tools. In addition, intranet blogs can serve as a training tool for new staff, coaching them on a new skill or marketing technique, for example. The intranet blog becomes an interactive forum for sharing experiences, judgments, and insights. Organizations that do not have the luxury of face-to-face training meetings but need to pass on knowledge to staff in various locations, will find that an intranet blog serves a valuable training function. E-mails and other documents always can be sent, but think of the benefit of having a living, breathing archive of all training materials.

Knowledge Management Blogs (K-Logs)

> Intranet blogs are great repositories for the intellectual property of any organization. An oft-quoted statistic is that "knowledge workers spend 35 percent of their productive time searching for information, while 40 percent of the corporate users report that they cannot find the information they need to do their jobs on their intranets."
> Working Council of CIOs

K-logs take information currently contained in many different locations throughout an organization ("silos") and place it all in one, easily accessed blog location. E-mails, documents, multimedia files, bookmark list links, and pictures are all examples of information types that can all be included in one location on a blog. K-logs also can absorb and post data drawn from external resources such as Web sites and RSS newsfeeds.

K-logs simplify finding information. Information is archived by category and date. In addition, quality blog platforms all contain search functionality. A K-log also can allow an individual to build a personal brand inside a company by demonstrating his or her expertise. Bloggers willing to share their expertise will find themselves the benefactors of openly expressed appreciation and thanks. Because blogs offer a built-in indicator of value and success, bloggers who have posts that share relevant information are linked to and read frequently and quickly achieve "name recognition." The ease and usability of K-logs will radically increase the likelihood that important information and knowledge *will* be captured and archived on the intranet.

Crisis Management

Blogs have a role to play in times of company crisis. In some ways, the communication features needed in a crisis are inherent in blogs. Situations where blogs might be used include crisis response and recovery during and following natural disasters such as those experienced on the Gulf Coast during hurricanes Katrina and Rita, financial and legal troubles, executive illness, anticorporate activists, or other public relations crises.

Managing a crisis often demands that information be updated and distributed to stakeholders on a frequent basis. The ability for information to be updated quickly, even immediately, is a feature blogs provide.

Blogs are excellent listening tools that allow companies to establish direct rapport with stakeholders. In addition, because blogs can be updated easily during a crisis, they enable instant two-way communication with stakeholders and create a public record of opinions and related facts that helps to minimize rumors and speculation. While blogs may not be the only tool needed to manage a crisis, they certainly have a place and should be a means of communication considered before a crisis ensues.

INTRANET BLOG PLATFORM REQUIREMENTS

In most cases, intranet blogging requires a somewhat different blog plat-form from that which may be needed for customer-focused blogs. First of all, they have to be password-protected and sit behind a firewall. Other-wise, they could be indexed by search engines and made available to the World Wide Web—not a good thing when sensitive company information is being posted. Security is the first matter to consider when determining which blog platform would be most appropriate in your situation.

Intranet blogs tend to be blog communities rather than single blogs. As such, a blog platform that supports multiple blogs is required. At the very least, the platform should be able to support multiple authors, if not multiple blogs.

When multiple blogs and bloggers are involved, it's best to have a platform that allows for complete editorial and administrative oversight. This enables the organization to determine to what level to monitor and screen content and comments submitted.

Reality Publisher by Blogging Systems, LLC (www.bloggingsystems .com), provides a platform that meets all the aforementioned needs. It is expressly suited to intranet environments and can manage large numbers of blogs and bloggers.

CONCLUSION

Intranet and knowledge-management blogs can serve organizations in a number of vital ways to help and encourage knowledge transfer inside the organization and contribute to a healthy workflow. They provide a means for instant content sharing, effective flow of strategic information and knowledge, and seamless access to information throughout an organ-ization. They contribute to a well-informed workforce and are a means to "capture" the knowledge of senior staff. In addition, their cost-effectiveness and ease of use put them within the reach of all organiza-tions both large and small.

Postscript

Realtors throughout the United States are already using blogs successfully to supercharge their marketing! We suggest that *now* is the time for *you* to implement the ideas and strategies outlined in this book—to take advantage of blogs as *the* most effective real estate marketing tool available today.

Here are some ways to get started:

- Go to our free blog platform, www.realtyblogging.com, and create your own personalized, individual blog. It takes less than 15 minutes to set up a blog at our site, and you can start experimenting with your "blog voice" to see how it feels. After just a few posts, you should become comfortable with your style of writing and get into the flow of things. Write with a local flavor in mind. Remember, you can compete against the national companies and new-age technology providers by keeping your content fresh, interesting, and local in nature.
- Start reading real estate-related blogs and commenting on what you find. The best way to jump-start your online reputation is to get involved and participate in the online conversation. Soon you will create friendships and associations that over time will result in goodwill and new business. As an example, Paul and I have gone from blogging about our own personal interests for a blog network for almost no pay to running the most successful blogging company in the real estate industry. We joined forces as a result of our meeting only through blogging. Blogging can have a similarly important impact for you, whether it is an increase in your client base or some new, unexpected direction in your real estate career.

- Think about creating a community blog that can supercharge your network marketing. Create *the* destination site for your local neighborhood by inviting local contributors such as the Chamber of Commerce, local charities, visitor bureaus, economic development entities, and other similar institutions to participate with you in writing about your community. Community Publisher from Blogging Systems (www.bloggingsystems.com) is the most advanced tool available to use for this purpose.
- Find additional support material regarding effective blog marketing at "Realty Blogging" (www.realtyblogging.com), a blog serving as "A network of blogging evangelists writing on effective real estate blogging." The blog's expert panel writes daily about effective blogging techniques, trends, tips, and tools that can be put into practice as agents learn how to use their blog efficiently. In addition, check our Web site, www.realtybloggingbook.com, for regular updates on the best tools for effective blog marketing.
- Review Appendices A, B, and C for basic information to help you get started.

Most Realtors still perceive their business as an offline one—if you start blogging *today,* there is a good chance that you will be the first in your target market. Any Realtor who blogs locally about his or her business will receive fantastic results that will get even better over time. Early adopters will be the ones that benefit from more links, more fresh content for the search engines to index, and more readers, leading to more clients. The opportunity to take advantage of blogging is *now.* This is especially the case if you create a community blog. Only one community blog is likely to dominate your target market. Anyone starting after you will find it hard to supplant your leadership position. In this industry, at this time, *the first-mover advantage is real*—make that move now and solidify yourself as the blogger of record for your market.

Richard Nacht

When it comes down to it, blogging is best done when it comes from the heart. It is, by its very nature, a personal means of expression. As a blogger, you must have passion for the topics about which you write—a "fire in the belly"—if you are going to be successful. You can take all the techniques we have taught you about the use of keywords, blog writing styles, or ways to position yourself as an expert, but if you lack passion, it will come to naught. It is form without substance, and that won't last very long.

Let me encourage you to find what ignites your passion and start there. My hope is that blogging will release a creative spark that will serve to energize, excite, and stimulate growth—both personally and professionally. For certain, it will enable you to get in touch with those things that matter most to you in business and in life.

Finally, let me heartily encourage you to participate in the greater conversation going on at all times in the blogosphere. It is a world that never sleeps. Perhaps even better than blogging personally is the benefit you can experience from interacting with other bloggers who share similar passions. I urge you to begin the journey into blogging. This is the only way that you will ever know the many wonderful benefits that will certainly come as a result. Your business will grow, and so will you.

I hope to meet you somewhere in the blogosphere—soon.

Paul Chaney

Afterword

I have received an unbelievable amount of business from my blog.
Ralph Roberts, *Time Magazine*'s Realtor of the Year

I was in real estate before cell phones, faxes, Web sites, and the Internet, but I have managed to adapt to all those things and others. Currently, the best way to build your business, create interest, drive traffic to your Web site, and continue the YOU, Inc., is blogging.

Why do I make such a claim? My own experiences with blogging have proven beyond a shadow of a doubt that it is a marketing approach that needs to be in every Realtor's toolkit.

As you may know, for the past two years I have been talking about real estate and mortgage fraud on my "Flipping Frenzy" blog (www. flippingfrenzy.com). I started using the blog merely as a way to get more information about the issue into the public domain. I was tired of media not picking it up and concluded that education was the key to curbing the problem.

It was not long after starting my blog that amazing things began to happen. The media started visiting the blog and began to use me as a source for feature articles on the subject. The FBI started referring people to the blog, and judges used it in two separate cases. As a result, I am now considered an international expert on mortgage fraud.

I have been asked by the producers of ABC's *Super Nanny* television show to do one on real estate. and thanks to blogging, I am now writing a book entitled, *Flipping Frenzy*. Further, I have been given the opportunity to be a keynote speaker at many top-level real estate conferences and events.

This is just the beginning of the benefits I have accrued both personally and professionally from the use of this medium. Blogging truly has taken my career and competitive differentiation to the next level. Talk about a branding tool! I realize now that I should have started even sooner and incorporated blogging into every aspect of my career. I wonder how many real estate customers I missed by not having a "Ralph Roberts Real Estate" blog. I do know that time and again clients have told me that one of the reasons they chose me as their real estate professional was because of the level of trust and expertise they sensed from regularly reading my blog.

Why do I tout my own blog success? Because what has worked for me will work for you!

I firmly believe that blogging should be at the top of everyone's marketing list. It provides a low-cost way of being out there in the marketplace every day. I project that in the next five years, 250,000 real estate agents could be blogging. Out of that number, 2,500 or so will lock up their own market where they are the expert. Will you be among that number? Blogging will be around a long time, but *now* is the time to get on board or get left behind. By following the suggestions and ideas outlined by Richard and Paul in this book, you can be assured that home buyers and sellers in your target market will come to your blog and not that of your competition and, as a result, will become your clients.

Ralph Roberts

APPENDIX

A

Ten Things to Consider Before You Start to Blog

In this book we have gone into great detail about the many benefits blogging can help you to accrue. There are some things to consider, however, before engaging in this exciting new marketing model.

1. Determine why you want to use a blog.

Have some sense of your specific purpose. For example, are you using the blog as a marketing channel, or will it be more for company news and updates? Do not do it because it is the latest Internet trend (notice that we did not say *fad*) or just because everyone else is doing it. We have outlined 10 specific benefits to using blogs. Before engaging in the practice of blogging, we strongly recommend assessing which of those would be applicable to you.

2. Consider your blog's core message and tone.

What are you going to write about? What topics will be covered? What "tone" will you give the blog? Should it be warm and humorous or more straightforward and informational? Your approach will be determined largely by the audience you are attempting to target. Obviously, when writing any blog, your primary consideration needs to be your readers (at least the readers you hope to attract).

3. Identify who is going to write the blog.

Blogs take time and forethought. They need someone who understands how to write "blog style." Invariably, the blogger will inject his or her personality. If this is you, be prepared to spend some time finding your "blog voice." If the blog is your company blog, it is incumbent upon you to find a writer who understands what makes your company tick and can reflect its persona accurately.

4. Determine whether you are prepared to engage in conversation without attempting to control the communication.

The blogosphere is a no-holds-barred, free-for-all means of communicating. It is often a two-way street. Readers can respond to what you have written using the "comments" option built into most blog platforms. Their responses may not always be kind. Not every organization is prepared for raw, unedited content to show up on its public Web site (blog).

Several options are available. You can choose to leave the comments feature turned off. However, this is not the best course of action to take. The beauty of blogs is that they are designed for interaction. Blogs are all about conversations between the blogger and readers. To turn comments off is to say to readers, "We don't value your input."

A second option is to prevent negative comments from reaching the public blog. However, that is less than optimal as well. Not only does it smack of controlling the communication, but it also is an attempt to sanitize your blog, purging it of what might prove to be valuable commentary. It will not take readers long to catch on to this and view it as a feigned public relations ploy, the result being that they do not come back.

The best way to approach this issue is to take each comment at face value. If it's obvious the commenter is just trying to "flame" you (unwarranted criticism), then screen the comment and prevent it from reaching the blog site. However, if the comment is salient and addresses a real issue, it is in your best interest to respond accordingly, giving the commenter the benefit of the doubt.

If you do not wish to reply on the blog itself, respond to the commenter via e-mail and tell him or her that you value the feedback. (Most blog platforms will send you a copy of the comment in an e-mail along with the person's e-mail address to which you can hit the "Reply" button and respond easily.) Open a dialogue. If you are successful, you will turn an enemy into a friend. Then go to your blog and talk about how you worked with the person to turn things around. Maybe even include a quote from that person. The message such action sends to readers is invaluable. It tells them that you have a sincere, genuine desire to serve their needs. Your willingness to be transparent about your interactions provides public relations value to which no dollar figure could ever be assigned!

5. Establish a company blogging policy with posting guidelines.

Susannah Gardner's book, *Buzz Marketing with Blogs for Dummies,* contains an entire section on this subject, including such specific guidelines as

- I will be accurate. When I make a mistake, I will correct it as quickly as possible.
- I will post only on the following topics: [list your topics].
- I will respond to comments and e-mails quickly.

6. Monitor what is being said about your company and your industry.

There are a number of reasons to do this, with the most obvious one being to find out how people view your company. You may find that no one is talking about you at all or that what is being said has negative or positive connotations. If you are not being talked about, even to a small degree, a blog can help to change that. If your company is being viewed negatively, you can use a blog to challenge misperceptions.

In addition, monitoring your industry helps you to know what is being said about your competitors. Observing industry trends might help you to find a niche worth exploiting or a marketing avenue others are overlooking. Many online tools have been created to assist you, such as

BlogPulse, Bloglines Citations, Technorati, PubSub, and IceRocket, to name a few. Google searches for your name and/or your company name also can help you to track this information.

7. Decide on a blog platform.

This is not difficult because many good platforms are available. (See Appendix B for more information on which blog platform is best for you.)

8. Identify ways to market your blog.

If the blog has marketing ramifications, getting the attention of search engines is vital. There are a variety of ways to do this, including submitting the blog to a number of search engines and blog directories. (Review Chapter 2 and Appendix D.)

9. Develop a plan to track statistics.

This is an area where bloggers traditionally have not paid much attention. However, when using blogs for marketing purposes, it is vital to know the effect they are having on your bottom line. Blogs are just like any other Web site in that their effect should be tracked in terms of unique visitors, page views, and conversion rates.

10. Be sure to know your keywords.

Blogs can help customers find your business when they are searching on Google or other sites. Therefore, it is important to know what words customers use most often to find you via the search engines and what words show up in competitor or industry blogs on a regular basis that help to place them high in Google's index.

Knowing which words to drop into your posts on a regular basis will help to boost your search rankings. Writing frequent, keyword-optimized entries can help to boost search standings, which goes a long way for a business owner on a tight marketing budget. Do not overdo it, though. Readers will see right through any obvious attempts at self-promotion, and search engines will penalize you for what they refer to as *keyword stuffing*.

APPENDIX
B

Choosing the Right Blog Platform

There are more than 50 blog platforms on the market today. Most provide similar functionalities. Some require more technical expertise than others, and as such, it is important that you find one that provides the best fit based on your technical skills and budget. Here is a review of several of the more popular blog platforms and details as to their advantages and disadvantages.

SINGLE-BLOG PLATFORMS

Blogger (www.blogger.com)

Blogger was one of the earliest blog platforms to be developed and has been credited with being the one that really helped to bring blogging to the masses. It is without question the most popular platform in use today.

Blogger is extremely easy to set up and use. Within just a few minutes, following a simple three-step process, you can have a blog online and ready to go. The interface is very intuitive and offers both WYSIWYG (What You See Is What You Get) and HTML (HyperText Markup Language) editing options. In other words, it requires no knowledge of HTML, but if you have some, you can click the "Edit HTML" tab and work with the source code itself. The platform also offers several attractive templates that you can switch to at your leisure. If you have the skills, you also can integrate the platform into your own Web site, thereby branding it with your own look and feel.

Blogger is free to use. But this comes with a price, albeit not a monetary one. Because Blogger is what is known as a *hosted platform*, every blog in its system has a search bar at the top of the page that links to Google (Blogger is owned by Google) and a series of buttons, including one that links the reader to other blogs in the network. The chief disadvantage to using Blogger is that it lacks some of the basic blog functionalities found on other platforms.

In our opinion, Blogger is an entry-level platform designed more for personal use.

Typepad (www.typepad.com)

Typepad is also a hosted solution and, like Blogger, is very easy to use, although not quite as intuitive. It is very popular with both personal and business users.

Typepad is not a free solution, but the fee is minimal, as little as $4.95 per month for the basic option and $14.95 per month for the pro version. If you pay a year in advance, you may get additional savings. The pro version offers the user the ability to create an unlimited number of individual blogs. (Typepad recently rolled out a version of its platform designed specifically for business use, but at almost $90 per month per blog, it is very expensive).

Typepad offers all the functionalities you would expect to find in a blog platform, including the ability for readers to leave comments, syndication of your content via Really Simple Syndication (RSS), and archiving of content by category and date. Placing images in a blog post is simple and is one of Typepad's most salient features.

Until recently, Typepad's design templates were somewhat lackluster and demanded quite a bit of customization to make them aesthetically pleasing. However, Typepad has added a number of new templates that are quite attractive, rivaling those found in Blogger.

Customizing the platform to *somewhat* resemble the look and feel of your Web site is easy to do. You can set colors and fonts to reflect those used on your site. You can upload a banner graphic in the header. However, matching the site design exactly will require extensive knowledge of HTML and Cascading Style Sheets (CSS), which means that you may need to hire a Web designer with specific blog knowledge.

Both Blogger and Typepad are targeted primarily toward personal users. If you want a platform specifically designed for business use, then the following are worth considering.

Movable Type (www.movabletype.org)

This platform is Typepad's elder sibling. Both are products offered by SixApart (*www.sixapart.com*) and are the result of the company's effort to reach both the personal and business markets.

Movable Type, or MT as it is often referred to, does require some HTML knowledge. The posting interface lacks full WYSIWYG capability, although it does offer some. If you want to use a bulleted or numbered list, for example, you will have to know the HTML code for those. In addition, inserting images is not nearly as simple and requires several steps.

Unlike Blogger or Typepad, Movable Type is a server-side platform. In other words, it sits on your own server and requires the help of either your server administrator or information technology (IT) staff to deploy and configure. (*Authors' caution:* Just because someone has technical knowledge does not always mean that they understand the inner workings of MT. We recommend hiring someone who has experience with the platform to install and configure it.)

MT does not come with a built-in set of templates, although prebuilt templates can be downloaded from the Internet. It is designed to be customized to match your Web site template and can be built within your Web site, although this also requires someone with experience to implement. The platform is available for commercial use for a one-time fee of $199 for up to five users.

WordPress (www.wordpress.org)

This platform is one we highly recommend. It is easier to use than Movable Type and is free. Like Movable Type, it also requires someone with technical knowledge to install and configure. Because WordPress is built using the open-source scripting language known as PHP, it is designed primarily to be used with Linux servers. (It can work on Windows servers, but this would require extra development time to configure.) Blogging Systems, LLC (www.bloggingsystems.com), is one of many companies that can create and implement a WordPress blog for Realtors.

WordPress offers WYSIWYG capability for creating posts. However, those who know HTML can opt for posting using HTML tags if they choose. Anyone familiar with Microsoft Word would have no difficulty using the platform. It is worth mentioning that WordPress does offer a hosted version as well, similar to Typepad or Blogger. It is free to use and can be found at WordPress.com.

Realty Blogging(www.realtyblogging.com)

Blogging Systems, LLC, offers Realtors a free blog at its "Realty Blogging" site (*www.realtyblogging.com*). Because this free blog resides within one of Blogging Systems full community blogs, the interface is easy to use and offers a more robust set of features than any individual blog platform available. (More detailed instructions on starting your free RealtyBlogging.com blog can be found in Appendix C.)

COMMUNITY BLOG PLATFORM

Blogging Systems, LLC (www.bloggingsystems.com)

For those interested in creating a community blog (multiple blogs networked through a central portal), there is no better option than that offered by Blogging Systems, LLC. Community Publisher and other related platforms offered are designed expressly for the purpose of building blog communities which allow you to host not only your own blog but the blogs of other groups, associations and organizations. The interface is easy to use and offers the most robust set of features of any platform available.

APPENDIX
C

Step-by-Step Guide to Creating Your Own Blog

This appendix will enable you to create your own blog in less than 15 minutes using the free real estate blog service from Realty Blogging (www.realtyblogging.com). This is and will be your own real estate blog, is free of charge, and will be available to you for your ongoing use.

To start, please open a Web browser page and enter this Uniform Resource Locator (URL) into the address box:

http://www.realtyblogging.com

Then
1. Click on the "Start Your Free Blog Here" link at the top right corner of the page.
2. Complete the fields on the "Start Your Free Blog Here" page, and click "Submit." (You will receive an e-mail with your login information for future reference.) You will be redirected to the administrative console to begin posting to your blog.
3. Click "New Post" on the "Quick Hits" sidebar on the right-hand side of the page (Figure C-1).

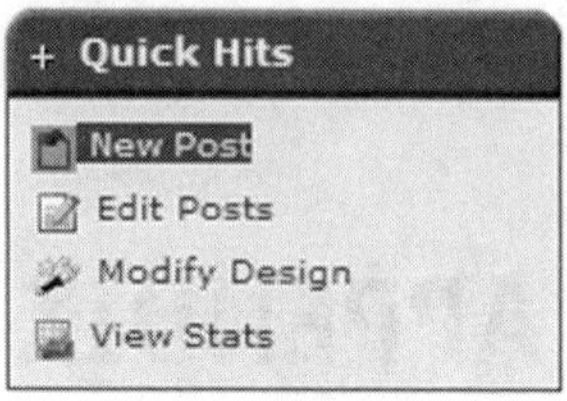

Figure C-1. Quick Hits.

Figure C-2. Title.

Figure C-3. Post status drop-down menu.

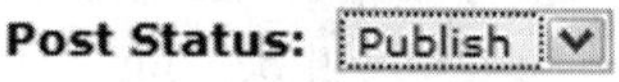

Figure C-4. Post status set to Publish option.

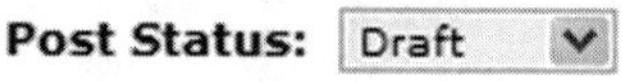

Figure C-5. Post status set to Draft option.

4. Type the title of your post into the "Title" field (Figure C-2).

5. Select the "Posting Status" using the drop-down menu. (By default, it is set to "Publish," which makes the post live immediately.) You can choose "Draft" to save it for further editing. For now, we suggest that you choose "Draft" because you can always return to your post and publish it (Figures C-3 through C-5).

6. Type your message (blog post) into the "Detail Content" field. Use the "Enter" key on your keyboard to start a new

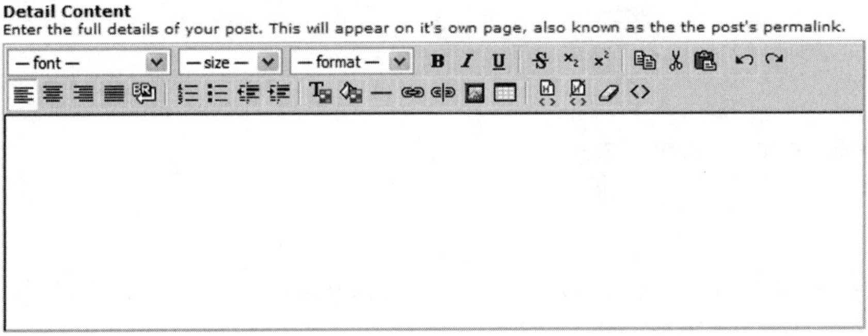
Detail Content
Enter the full details of your post. This will appear on it's own page, also known as the the post's permalink.
— font —
— size —
— format —

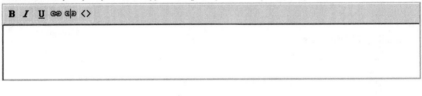

Figure C-6. Detail Content field.

Summary
Enter a summary for your post. It will appear along with your title in your list of posts.

Figure C-7. Post Summary field.

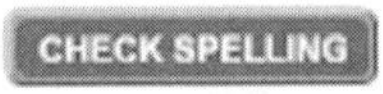
CHECK SPELLING

Figure C-8. Spell Check button.

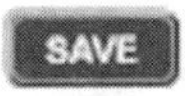
SAVE

Figure C-9. Save button.

paragraph. Feel free to use the "MS Word-type" toolbar to customize your content (Figure C-6).

7. Create a summary of your message using the "Summary" field. If you wish, this summary simply could be the opening few sentences of your post (Figure C-7).
8. Check spelling using the "Spell Check" button (optional) (Figure C-8).

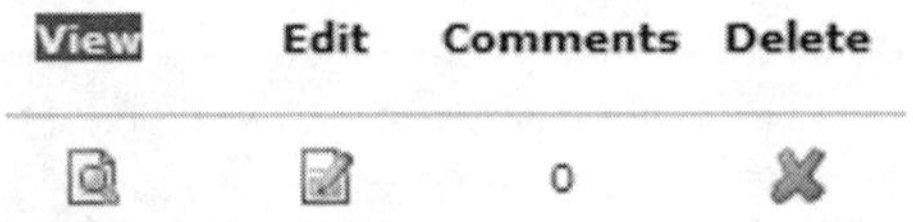

| View | Edit | Comments | Delete |

Figure C-10. Click "View Blog" link.

Title: Your Post Title Goes Here   **Post Date:** 5/30/2006 10:23:00
Post Status: Publish ▾

| Content | Categories | Images | Attachments | Options | Manage Comments |

Add A New Personal Category

[   ] ADD

Existing Categories

⊙ Community

☐ Realty Blogging - The Book

☐ Effective Blog Marketing

☑ Real Estate Bloggers

Figure C-11. Blog post categories.

Title: Your Post Title Goes Here   **Post Date:** 5/30/2006 13:46:00
Post Status: Publish ▾

| Content | Categories | Images | Attachments | Options | Manage Comments |

Generate Photo Album: ☐

Display Order   Image

⊤ ↑ ↓ ⊥

Figure C-12. Add images to post.

9. Click "Save" to publish your post (or save as a draft, as noted earlier) (Figure C-9).

10. Click the "View" link at the top of the page to see your new blog (Figure C-10).

If you chose "Draft" as your "Posting Status" in step 5, your post is not yet available for public view. If you like the way your post appears, you can return to step 10 and click on "Edit." When the next page appears, change the "Posting Status" to "Publish," and then click on the "Save" button. Your post is now public for the world to see.

OPTIONAL STEPS

11. Assign your post to community and personal categories by clicking on the "Category" tab. Then click on the community and personal drop-down buttons and assign your post by checking the applicable boxes (Figure C-11).

12. Add images to your post by clicking on the "Images" tab (Figure C-12).

Add images to your post by browsing and selecting the image from your folder and entering a caption and its display order.

APPENDIX

D

Best Directories for Real Estate Marketing Purposes

Real estate blogs are exploding on the Web. From almost none as recently as 2005, it is estimated that there are now thousands, with new ones being created every day. For additional exposure on the Web, Figures D-1 to D-29 show good blog directories for submitting your own blog.

Figure D-1. www.blog-search.com

Figure D-2. www.blogarama.com

Figure D-3. www.blogcatalog.com

Figure D-4.   www.blogdex.net

Figure D-5.   www.blogdigger.com

Figure D-6.   www.blogexplosion.com

BLOGFINDS.com

Figure D-7.   www.blogfinds.com

Figure D-8.   www.blogflux.com

BLOGGERNITY
Blogger Search Directory

Figure D-9.   www.bloggernity.com

Figure D-10.   www.bloghop.com

Figure D-11. www.blogpulse.com

Figure D-12. www.blogrankings.com

blogtagstic

Figure D-13. www.blogtagstic.com

Figure D-14. www.blogtopsites.com

Bloogz
World Wide Blog

Figure D-15. www.bloogz.com

blogwise

Figure D-16. www.blogwise.com

Figure D-17. www.sarthak.net/blogz/index.php

Figure D-18.　www.contentsmatter.com

Figure D-19.　www.dmoz.org/add.html

Figure D-20.　www.getblogs.com

Figure D-21.　www.globeofblogs.com

Figure D-22.　www.icerocket.com

Figure D-23.　http://portal.eatonweb.com

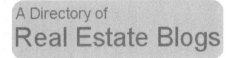

Figure D-24. www.real-estate-blogs.com/blogs/

Figure D-25. www.realtyfeedsearch.com

Figure D-26. www.search4blogs.com

Figure D-27. www.technorati.com

Figure D-28. http://ecom.yahoo.com/dir/submit/intro/

Figure D-29. www.yourwebloghere.com

APPENDIX
E

Really Simple Syndication (RSS) and How to Use It

A companion technology used by virtually all blog platforms that helps to facilitate direct communication between you and your readers is something called *Really Simple Syndication* (RSS). It can provide an easy way to distribute news and updates, thus encouraging more traffic to your blog or Web site.

RSS DEFINED

RSS is an acronym that stands for, among other things, *Really Simple Syndication*. It is a format for syndicating Web site content such as might be found on major news sites such as CNN, as well as on blogs. The term used for such syndication is *RSS feed*. Blogs tend to be the most common type of site to use RSS, but any Web site that has routinely updated content can and should be RSS-enabled.

The reason you should consider syndicating your blog via RSS feeds is simply that it gives you yet another method for getting your message into the hands of consumers and others. As RSS gains in popularity (thanks to services such as MyYahoo! and MyMSN personalized portals, not to mention being incorporated into Vista, Microsoft's new operating system due out in 2007), it can have great implications for sales and marketing. One of the best features of RSS is that, unlike e-mail, users only receive content to which they have subscribed. Therefore, RSS is not subject to the same problems with spam or the need for spam filters as its e-mail counterpart.

It is likely that you have seen a small orange button on many Web sites with the term *RSS* or *XML*. That button has become an industry standard and identifies the site as RSS-enabled. Recently, there has been a move toward standardizing the RSS button to look like the button on the right:

RSS READERS/AGGREGATORS

If you click on the button (sometimes it is a text link), you often will see nothing more than a page of code. RSS is designed for software programs called *RSS readers* or *RSS aggregators.* These programs, of which there are many, interpret this code, enabling the reader to see the syndicated content.

HOW RSS WORKS

RSS works in the following manner: A user either downloads to his or her desktop or uses a Web-based RSS reader, which resembles an e-mail program's interface. Many such programs exist, but some of the more popular are

- *Newsgator (www.newsgator.com).* This is available in both a desktop version that integrates with Microsoft Outlook, making it both an e-mail client and an RSS reader in one, and a Web-based version. The desktop version is available at a cost of about $30, whereas the Web-based version is free.
- *Bloglines (www.bloglines.com).* This is a Web-based RSS reader that is also free.

- *Pluck (www.pluck.com).* This is a free desktop version that integrates either into Internet Explorer or Firefox browsers.

In addition, if you use MyYahoo!, MyMSN, or Google's personalized page as your home page you can easily incorporate feeds into them from your favorite blogs or news Web sites when you log on to your home page. In fact, you may even see MyYahoo! or MyMSN buttons on blogs that allow a simple one-click subscription to the feed. Figure E-1 is an example of such buttons. You will notice ones for MyYahoo!, MyMSN, Bloglines, and Newsgator, along with buttons for other feed readers as well.

Let's say you find an RSS-enabled site that contains content you want to read regularly. Using the RSS reader of your choice, you subscribe to the site's RSS feed. If the RSS-enabled site includes buttons such as the ones in the figure, all you need to do is click on the appropriate button corresponding to your RSS reader. Otherwise, you may have to copy the Uniform Resource Locator (URL) of the RSS-enabled page into your RSS reader. Once one or the other of these steps is taken, the aggregator will search the site periodically for updated content. This search can take place hourly, daily, or less often depending on the preference of the user.

Figure E-1. List of RSS feeds.

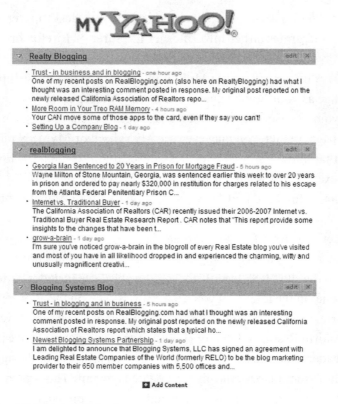

Figure E-2.   RSS feeds in MyYahoo!

When the program finds new content, it is pulled into the aggregator's interface for you to read. Some aggregators even notify you when
fresh content is available. Figure E-2 is a screen shot of a MyYahoo! RSS
reader.

Unlike e-mail, which is considered *push* technology in that the user
has to wait for a message to be broadcast before he or she receives it, RSS
is *pull* technology. This means that the aggregator is constantly searching
for updates and delivering them to the user within the time frame the user
establishes.

RSS is a huge convenience for anyone who spends time doing
research on the Internet. Instead of going from site to site to find new
information, RSS literally brings it to your door! Not only can you subscribe to a given site's feed, but you can also subscribe to RSS-feed key-

word searches on Google and Yahoo!, as well as other engines. They are all now RSS-enabled.

Not only is RSS useful for individuals, but it also can help to bring life back to a site gone stale. RSS feeds can be used to import fresh content for use on almost any Web site. Imagine the benefit this provides to a static Web site when, for example, constantly updated company news headlines can be incorporated.

Although RSS is still a mystery to many people, it is a technology that you should embrace. It is another way to get your message directly to people who want to read it, increase traffic, and build greater brand awareness.

(*Authors' note:* While it's possible to pull RSS feeds into a blog in order to populate it with fresh content, this is not considered a best practice. Blogs should be updated with original content whenever possible.)

Index